Weight Watchers
Freestyle Meal Prep 2019

Selected and Mots Delicious WW Smart points Recipes to Lose Weight, Reclaim Your Health and Energy with 30-Day Meal Plan – Lose Up to 30 Pounds in 30 Days

By

Briana Mckenna

Copyright © **Briana Mckenna** 2019

All rights reserved. No part of this publication maybe reproduced, stored or transmitted in any form or by any means, electronic, mechanical, photocopying, recording, scanning, or otherwise without written permission from the author. It is illegal to copy this book, post it to a website, or distribute it by any other means without permission.

Briana Mckenna the moral right to be identified as the author of this work.

Table of Contents

Introduction 5

30 Days Weight Watchers Meal Plan 6

   Day 1 6

   Day 2 9

   Day 3 12

   Day 4 15

   Day 5 18

   Day 6 21

   Day 7 23

   Day 8 24

   Day 9 28

   Day 10 30

   Day 11 32

   Day 12 35

   Day 13 37

   Day 14 40

   Day 15 42

   Day 16 45

   Day 17 47

   Day 18 49

   Day 19 52

   Day 20 54

   Day 21 56

   Day 22 59

Day 23... 61
Day 24... 64
Day 25... 66
Day 26... 69
Day 27... 71
Day 28... 74
Day 29... 77
Day 30... 79
Conclusion 82

Introduction

Weight watchers is a lifestyle that you can stay on to maintain a healthy weight. You have to allow enough time to be successful because there are many people who quit plans to early and they do not get the benefit of reaching there weight loss goals.

People follow Weight Watchers since it has a simple approach to losing weight. You need to learn how to control your appetite and to beat temptation. You eat filling foods so you will eat less. You learn to make smart choices. You rely on the plan; choose with your points system. Then you adapt the plan to fit your lifestyle. This is a new approach to eating.

If you are looking for a plan with a little flexibility but still will get you the end result of healthy weight loss and a slimmer you, give Weight Watchers a try. Combining its eating regimen with any workout or regular exercise, you will see excellent results.

30 Days Weight Watchers Meal Plan

Day 1

BREAKFAST: KETO SAUSAGE BREAKFAST SANDWICH

Prep Time: 5mins, Total Time: 15mins, Serves: 2

Ingredients:

- 6 - large eggs
- 2 - tbsp. heavy cream
- Pinch red pepper flakes
- Kosher salt
- Freshly ground black pepper
- 1 - tbsp. butter
- 3 - slices cheddar
- 6 - frozen sausage patties, heated according to package instructions
- Avocado, sliced

Instructions:

1. In a little bowl beat eggs, overwhelming cream, and red pepper chips altogether. Season liberally with salt and pepper.
2. In a nonstick skillet over medium warmth, liquefy margarine. Pour roughly ⅓ of the eggs into the skillet.
3. Place a cut of cheddar in the center and let take a seat around 1 minute. Overlay the edges of the egg into the center, ensuring the cheddar.
4. Expel from dish and rehash with outstanding eggs.
5. Serve eggs between two wiener patties with avocado.

Nutrition information: calories 160g: fat 10.3g, carbohydrate 3.2g, sugar 14g, protein 18.7g. Points Value Per serving: 08

LUNCH: TURKEY SAUSAGE FRITTATA

Prep Time: 10mins, Total Time: 40mins, Serves: 8

Ingredients:

- 12 - oz ground breakfast sausage, turkey
- 2 - bell peppers
- 12 - eggs
- 1 - cup lactose free sour cream
- 1 - tsp pink Himalayan salt
- 1 - tsp black pepper
- 2 - tsp Kerry Gold butter

- optional 2-oz shredded Tillamook cheddar

Instructions

1. Preheat your stove to 350F.
2. Break every one of your eggs into a blender; include the acrid cream, salt and pepper. Mix on high for 30 seconds. Put aside.
3. Warmth a huge skillet on medium warmth. With regards to temperature include the margarine.
4. Cut your chime peppers into strips. Add it to the skillet. Sauté until seared and delicate around 6 minutes.
5. Expel the peppers from the skillet.
6. Rapidly include the turkey frankfurter and blend, separating the meat until seared, around 8 minutes. Smooth the turkey to the base of the skillet.
7. Include the peppers over it, uniformly disseminated. Pour the egg blend over everything.
8. Place the skillet in the broiler and heat for 30 minutes. In the event that you need to include the cheddar, sprinkle it over the frittata when you remove it from the stove so it liquefies.

Nutrition Information: Calories 240g: Fat 16.7g, Carbohydrate 5.5g, Sugar 18g, Protein 16.7g, **Points Value Per serving: 7.5**

DINNER: LOW CARB KETO LASAGNA

Prep Time: 10mins, Total Time: 55mins , Serve: 6,
Ingredients:

- 1 - tablespoon butter, ghee, coconut oil, or lard
- ½ - lb spicy Italian sausage or sweet Italian sausage
- 15 -oz ricotta cheese
- 2 - tablespoons coconut flour
- medium-high large whole egg
- 1 ½ - teaspoon salt
- ½ - teaspoon pepper
- 1 - teaspoon garlic powder
- a large clove garlic finely chopped
- 1 ½ - cup mozzarella cheese
- 1/3 - cup parmesan cheese
- 4 large zucchini's sliced long ways to ¼ pieces
- 16 -oz. Rao's marinara sauce
- 1 - tablespoon mixed Italian herb seasoning
- ¼ to ½ - tsp red pepper flake
- ¼ - cup basil

Instructions:

1. Warmth 1 tablespoon of spread or fat of decision in a monstrous skillet over medium-high warmth.
2. Separate and diminish shaded Italian wiener. Remove from the sparkle and let cool.
3. Preheat stove to 375 degrees and coat a 9×9 warming dish with a cooling shower or spread.
4. Fuse ricotta cheddar, 1 extent of mozzarella cheddar, 2 tablespoons of parmesan cheddar.
5. Add 1 egg, coconut flour, salt, garlic, garlic powder, and pepper to a little bowl and blend until smooth. Put aside.
6. Incorporate Italian enhancing and red pepper drops to a compartment of marinara, blend well. Set aside.
7. Incorporate a layer of sliced zucchini to the base of the lubed dish. Spread ¼ proportions of cheddar mix over zucchini, sprinkle with ¼ of the Italian sausage and a while later incorporate a layer of sauce.
8. Repeat process 3-4 times until the point when the moment that fixings are by and large gone, completing with a layer of sauce.
9. Incorporate residual mozzarella cheddar and sprinkle with remarkable parmesan cheddar.
10. Cover with foil and get ready for 30 minutes. Remove upset and get ready for an additional 15 minutes until splendid dim hued.
11. Oust from oven and let sit for 5-10 minutes before serving. Sprinkle with new basil if needed.

Nutrition Information: Calories 364g: Fat 21g, Carb 12g, Sugar 19g, Fiber 6g Protein 32g, **Points Value Per serving: 15**

Day 2

BREAKFAST: KETO PANCAKES

Prep Time: 5mins, Total Time: 15mins, Serves: 3

Ingredients:

- ½ - c. almond flour
- 4 - oz. cream cheese, softened
- 4 - large eggs
- 1 - tsp. lemon zest
- Butter, for frying and serving

Instructions:

1. In a nonstick skillet over medium warmth, condense 1 tablespoon spread.
2. In a medium bowl, whisk together almond flour, cream cheddar, eggs, and lemon get-up-and-go until smooth.
3. Pour in around 3 tablespoons hitter and cook until splendid, 2 minutes.
4. Flip and cook 2 minutes more. Trade to a plate and continue with whatever is left of the hitter.
5. Serve completed with spread.

Nutrition Information: Calories 240.4g: Fat 17.2g, Carbohydrate 11.7g, Sugars 1.3g, Fiber 6.5g, Protein 9.6g, **Points Value Per serving: 11**

LUNCH: BUFFALO CHICKEN CASSEROLE

Prep time: 10mins, Total time: 35mins, Serves: 4-6

Ingredients:

- 2½ - cups shredded chicken
- 3 - cups riced cauliflower
- 1½ - cups monterey jack cheese
- 1½ - cups sharp cheddar cheese
- ¾ - cup greek yogurt, sour cream or mayo
- 2 - cups yellow onion, chopped
- 2 - cups carrot/broccoli slaw, chopped
- 1 - cup kale, finely chopped
- 1 - cup bell pepper (red, yellow, orange), chopped
- 1 - tbsp garlic
- 1 - tbsp olive oil
- 2 - tbsp butter, melted
- ¼ - ½ cup hot sauce
- salt and pepper, to taste

For topping:

- Avocado slices
- green onions
- tomatoes
- bell pepper
- sour cream
- Yogurt.

Instructions:

1. Add olive oil to a container over medium high warmth. Include onion and cook for around five minutes, mixing periodically so it doesn't consume.
2. Include carrot/broccoli slaw, chime pepper and garlic, cook for an additional three minutes. Include kale and cook until the point when kale has withered around 2-3 minutes.
3. In a heating dish (9x9 for taller, 9x13 for more slender), include the liquefied spread and Greek yogurt (or sharp cream or mayo).
4. Combine well (least demanding to do with a fork or a whisk). At that point include destroyed chicken. Coat chicken in yogurt/hot sauce blend.
5. Include onion, carrot, kale, chime pepper blend. Consolidate well. Include cauliflower or spaghetti squash noodles and consolidate well once more.
6. Include half of the cheddar, consolidate well. Top with outstanding cheddar.
7. Cook at 375 for 15 minutes until the point that cheddar is bubbly to finish everything. You can likewise sear for around 5 minutes on the off chance that you'd like.
8. Top with your most loved fixings. I utilized Avocado cuts, red chime pepper and Green Onions.

Nutrition Information: Calories 342.5g: Fat 9.4g, Carbohydrate 47.8g, Sugars 8.2g, Fiber 2.8g, Protein 16.8g, **Points Value Per serving: 15**

DINNER: LOADED CAULIFLOWER BAKE

Prep Time: 15mins, Total Time: 1hr, Serve: 4

Ingredients:

- 1 expansive head cauliflower, cut into florets
- 2 tbsp. spread
- 1 container overwhelming cream
- 2 oz. cream cheddar
- 1 1/4 container destroyed sharp cheddar, isolated
- Salt and pepper to taste
- 6 cuts bacon, cooked and disintegrated
- 1/4 container hacked green onions

Instructions:

1. Preheat broiler to 350 degrees.
2. In a vast pot of bubbling water, whiten cauliflower florets for 2 minutes. Deplete cauliflower.
3. In a medium pot, soften together margarine, substantial cream, cream cheddar, 1 measure of destroyed cheddar, salt, and pepper until very much joined.
4. In a preparing dish, include cauliflower florets, cheddar sauce, everything except 1 tbsp. disintegrated bacon, and everything except 1 tbsp. green onions. Blend together.
5. Top with staying destroyed cheddar disintegrated bacon and green onions.
6. Prepare until the point that cheddar is bubbly and brilliant and cauliflower is delicate around 30 minutes.
7. Serve quickly and appreciate

Nutrition Information: Calories 498g: Fat 45g, Carbohydrate 5.8g, Protein 13.9g, **Points Value Per serving: 20**

Day 3

BREAKFAST: BELL PEPPER EGGS

Prep Time: 5mins, Total Time: 20mins, Serves: 3

Ingredients:

- 1 - bell pepper, sliced into 1/4" rings
- 6 - eggs
- kosher salt
- Freshly ground black peppers
- 2 - tbsp. Chopped chives
- 2 - tbsp. chopped parsley

Instructions:

1. Warmth a nonstick skillet over medium warmth, and oil softly with cooking splash.
2. Place a ringer pepper ring in the skillet, at that point sauté for two minutes. Flip the ring; at that point break an egg in the center.
3. Season with salt and pepper, at that point cook until the point when the egg is cooked to your loving, 2 to 4 minutes.
4. Rehash with alternate eggs, at that point embellish with chives and parsley.

Nutrition Information: Calories 121.5g: Fat 7.9g, Carbohydrate 4.0g, Sugars 0.0g, Fiber 1.0g, Protein 8.6g, **Points Value Per serving: 4.5**

LUNCH: COBB EGG SALAD

Prep Time: 10mins, Total Time: 20mins, Servings: 4 -6

Ingredients

- 6 - Large Phil's Fresh Eggs hard boiled and peeled
- 4 - pieces bacon cooked and chopped
- ¼ - c. diced grape tomatoes
- ¼ - c. chopped arugula
- ¼ - c. finely shredded cheddar cheese
- ¼ - c. crumbled blue cheese
- 6 - Tbsp. mayo
- 2 - tsp. dry ranch dressing mix

Instructions:
1. Hack eggs; include remaining fixings and mix delicately until blended.
2. Appreciate in a sandwich, with wafers, or all alone!

Nutrition Information: Calories 162g: Fat 9g, Carbohydrate 6.4g, Sugars 7.1g, Fiber 3.6g, Protein 6.7g, <u>**Points Value Per serving: 7**</u>

DINNER: CAULIFLOWER FRIED RICE

Prep Time: 5mins, Total Time: 30mins, Servings: 4

Ingredients:

- 1 - large head cauliflower
- 1 - large chicken breast
- 4 - eggs
- Salt
- Pepper
- ½ - cup diced carrots
- ½ - cup diced red bell pepper
- ½ - cup diced yellow bell pepper
- 4 - spring onions
- 2 - cloves garlic
- 2 - tsp grated ginger
- 1-2 - tsp of Amarillo
- 4 - Tbsp soy sauce

Instructions:

1. Warmth a substantial overwhelming base skillet that has a top over medium warmth.
2. Warmth a standard measured dish over medium warmth.
3. Salt and pepper chicken bosom on the two sides.
4. In a little bowl, whisk together 4 eggs with somewhat salt and pepper.
5. Once the vast skillet is extremely HOT (!) include a sprinkle of oil and afterward chicken bosom.
6. Sear for one moment, at that point turn, broil for one more moment, cover with a top and promptly decrease warmth to LOW, set a caution for 10 minutes (imperative!).
7. Add a sprinkle of oil to the HOT little dish and after that include whisked eggs and let cook like a hotcake. Around 2.5 minutes on one side and one more moment on the other.
8. Expel from dish when cooked through and cut into little squares.

9. Presently cut cauliflower into florets, wash, shake out well and add to a sustenance processor (I needed to do this in 3 sections in light of the fact that my nourishment processor is little).
10. Heartbeat until the point when you have rice corn estimated bits. Put aside.
11. At the point when chicken bosom caution goes off, expel the skillet from warm however don't lift the top. No looking! Simply expel from warmth and set another clock for an additional 10 minutes.
12. Peel carrots and cleave into corn part estimated pieces.
13. Wash and daintily cut the white piece of spring onions and place alongside carrots.
14. At that point cut green section somewhat thicker and put on the different corner of hacking board or in a little bowl.
15. Peel and mesh garlic and ginger and place alongside cleaved carrots.
16. Wash chime peppers and hack into corn part estimated pieces and place on the different end of cleaving load up or a little bowl.
17. When chicken bosom caution goes off once more, expel the chicken bosom from container and place on a hacking board.
18. Cut chicken into chickpea-sized squares.
19. Place the extensive skillet you utilized for the chicken bosom back on the burner and warmth over medium warmth.
20. Once hot, include a sprinkle of oil and include hacked carrots, white piece of onions, garlic, ginger and of Amarillo to the dish and panfry for around 2 minutes, at that point include cauliflower rice and slashed ringer pepper and stirfry for an additional 3 minutes, at that point include chicken, egg and soy sauce and stirfry for an additional 2 minutes.

Nutrition Information: Calories 99g: Fat 4g, Carb 7g, Sugars 2g, Fiber 1g, Protein 8g, **Points Value Per serving: 08**

Day 4

BREAKFAST: JALAPEÑO POPPER EGG CUPS

Prep Time: 15mins, Total Time: 35mins, Serves: 4 - 6

Ingredients:
- 12 - slices bacon
- 10 - large eggs
- ¼ - c. sour cream
- ½ - c. shredded Cheddar
- ½ - c. shredded mozzarella
- 2 - jalapeños, 1 minced and 1 thinly sliced
- 1 - tsp. garlic powder
- kosher salt
- Freshly ground black pepper
- nonstick cooking spray

Instructions:

1. Preheat broiler to 375°.
2. Put aside on a paper towel-lined plate to deplete.
3. In an extensive bowl, whisk together eggs, sharp cream, cheeses, minced jalapeño and garlic powder. Season with salt and pepper.
4. Utilizing nonstick cooking splash, oil a biscuit tin. Line each well with one cut of bacon, at that point empty egg blend into every biscuit glass until around 66% of the route to the best. Top every biscuit with a jalapeño cut.
5. Prepare for 20 minutes, or until the eggs never again look wet.
6. Cool somewhat before expelling from the biscuit tin. Serve.

Nutrition Information: Calories 86g: Fat 9.5g, Carbohydrates 2.5g, Sugars 1.3g, Fiber 0.6g, Protein 12.9g, **Points Value Per serving: 7**

LUNCH: HONEY MUSTARD CHICKEN SALAD WITH BACON & AVOCADO

Prep Time: 10mins, Total Time: 25mins, Servings: 4

Ingredients:

Dressing/ Marinade:
- 1/3 - cup honey
- 3 - tablespoons whole grain mustard
- 2 - tablespoons smooth and mild Dijon mustard
- 2 - tablespoons olive oil
- 1-2 - tablespoons Apple cider vinegar or white vinegar

- 1 - teaspoon minced garlic
- Salt to season
- 4 - skinless and boneless chicken thighs or chicken breasts

For Salad:

- ¼ - cup diced bacon, trimmed of rind and fat
- 4 - cups Romaine lettuce leaves, washed
- 1 - cup sliced grape or cherry tomatoes
- 1 - large avocado, pitted and sliced
- ¼ - cup corn kernels
- ¼ - of a red onion, sliced

Instructions:

1. Whisk marinade/dressing fixings together to join. Empty a large portion of the marinade into a shallow dish to marinade the chicken filets for two hours if time permits. Refrigerate the saved immaculate marinade to use as a dressing.
2. Warmth a nonstick container (or flame broil dish or skillet) over medium warmth with about a teaspoon of oil and burn/barbecue chicken filets on each side until brilliant, fresh and cooked through. (Flame broil in bunches to avert abundance water being discharged.) Once chicken is cooked, put aside and permit to rest.
3. Wipe dish over with paper towel; shower with another teaspoon of oil and broil the bacon until firm.
4. Cut chicken into strips and get ready plate of mixed greens with leaves, tomatoes, avocado cuts, corn, onion strips and chicken.
5. Whisk 2 tablespoons of water into the staying immaculate marinade/dressing and sprinkle over the serving of mixed greens.
6. Sprinkle the bacon over the best and season with some additional salt and split pepper

Nutrition Information: Calories 410g: Fat 20g, Carb 34g, Sugars 25g, Protein 25g, **Points Value Per serving: 22**

DINNER: RANCH CHICKEN AND VEGGIES

Serves: 4

Ingredients:

- 1 and ½ - pounds boneless chicken bosoms
- Assorted veggies to fill your skillet, cut into 1 inch pieces
- ½ - teaspoon dried parsley
- ½ - teaspoon dried dill
- ½ - teaspoon dried chives
- ½ - teaspoon garlic powder
- ½ - teaspoon onion powder
- ½ - teaspoon ocean salt
- pinch of dark pepper
- 3 - tablespoons ghee or margarine, liquefied

Optional for serving:

- hot sauce

Instructions:

1. Preheat stove to 400 degrees F.
2. Add chicken and veggies to a substantial sheet container - I line it with material paper for simple cleanup.
3. Combine the dried parsley, dill, chives, garlic powder, onion powder, ocean salt, and pepper and sprinkle over the chicken and veggies.
4. Next, shower your softened ghee or spread everywhere throughout the highest point of the chicken and veggies. This is what it would appear that before it goes in the stove:

Prepare for 35 - 45 minutes or until the point when chicken is cooked all through and the veggies are somewhat caramelized. Present with hot sauce, if wanted. Appreciate!

Nutrition Information: Calories 178.5g: Fat 1.9g, Carbohydrate 9.1g, Sugars 0.4g, Fiber 0.4g, Protein 28.3g, **Points Value Per serving: 7**

Day 5

BREAKFAST: KETO BREAKFAST CUPS

Prep Time: 15mins, Total Time: 40mins, Serves: 12

Ingredients:

- 2 - lb. ground pork
- 1 - tbsp. freshly chopped thyme
- 2 - cloves garlic, minced
- ½ - tsp. paprika
- ½ - tsp. ground cumin
- 1 - tsp. kosher salt
- Freshly ground black pepper
- 2 ½ - c. chopped fresh spinach
- 1 - c. shredded white cheddar
- 12 - eggs
- 1 - tbsp. freshly chopped chives

Instructions:

1. Preheat stove to 400°. In a vast bowl, consolidate ground pork, thyme, garlic, paprika, cumin, and salt. Season with pepper.
2. Include a little bunch of pork to every biscuit tin well at that point press up the sides to make a container.
3. Gap spinach and cheddar equally between mugs. Split an egg over each glass and season with salt and pepper.
4. Prepare for the point that eggs are set and wiener is cooked through around 25 minutes. Enhancement with chives and serve.

Nutrition Information: Calories 201.9g: Fat 14.5g, Carbohydrate 1.1g, Sugars 0.4g, Fiber 0.1g, Protein 15.8g, **Points Value Per serving: 9**

LUNCH: EASY HEALTHY TACO SALAD WITH GROUND BEEF

Prep Time: 10mins, Total Time: 20mins, Servings: 3

Ingredients:

- 1 - lb Ground beef
- 1 - tsp Avocado oil or any oil of choice
- 2 - tbsp Taco seasoning
- 8 - oz Romaine lettuce chopped
- 1 1/3 - cup Grape tomatoes halved
- ¾ - cup Cheddar cheese shredded
- 1 - medium Avocado cubed
- ½ - cup Scallions chopped
- 1/3 - cup Salsa
- 1/3 - cup Sour cream

Instructions:

1. Warmth oil in a skillet over high warmth. Include ground meat. Panfry, separating the pieces with a spatula, for around 7-10 minutes, until the point when the meat is caramelized and dampness has dissipated.
2. Blend taco flavoring into the ground hamburger until the point that very much joined.
3. In the mean time, consolidate every outstanding fixing in a huge bowl.
4. Include the ground meat. Hurl everything together.

Nutrition Information: Calories 560g: Fat 41g, Carbohydrates 6g, Sugars 6.2g, Fiber 3.1g, Protein 42g, **Points Value Per serving: 25**

DINNER: LOW CARB PHO VIETNAMESE BEEF NOODLE SOUP

Prep Time: 15mins, Total Time: 3hrs 15mins, Servings: 4-5

Ingredients:

- 6 - Meat bones browned and roasted - the more connective tissue, the better!
- ½ - Onion charred
- 1 - tablespoon Fresh Ginger sliced
- 1 - tbsp Salt
- 3 - tbsp Fish Sauce
- 2 - pods Star Anise
- 1 – gallon of Water
- 5 - packages Shirataki
- ¼ - pound Flank Steak raw, thinly sliced

- 1 - cup Bean Sprouts
- 5 - sprigs Thai Basil
- ½ - Jalapeno sliced
- ½ - Scallion chopped

Instructions:

1. Preheat oven to 425 degrees F.
2. Cover cheeseburger bones in water and rise for 15 minutes in an immense stockpot on the stovetop while the oven preheats.
3. Place parboiled cheeseburger bones and onion on a planning sheet or dinner dish and feast for 45 - 60 minutes
4. Let the bones and the onion sautéed and obscured.
5. Heave bones, onion, fresh ginger, salt, point sauce, star anise and new water into weight cooker.
6. Set the weight cooker to high weight for 2 hours. In case you are using a stovetop, you will stew for 6-8 hours.
7. Strain juices with a fine colander.
8. Place shirataki noodles and meat of choice in a bowl; void squeezes over the best into the bowl while it is still particularly hot.
9. Blend and let sit until the point that unrefined meat is never again pink and noodles are cooked 1 to 2 minutes.
10. Present with fixings and veggies of choice as a bit of hindsight.

Nutrition Information: Calories 172g: Fat 5g, Carb 3g, Sugars 1g, Protein 25g, **Points Value Per serving: 4**

Day 6

BREAKFAST: OMELET STUFFED PEPPERS

Prep Time: 15mins, Total Time: 1 hour 0mins, Serves: 4

Ingredients:

- 2 - bell peppers, halved (seeds removed)
- 8 - eggs, lightly beaten
- ¼ - c. milk
- 4 - slices bacon, cooked and crumbles
- 1 - c. shredded Cheddar
- 2 - tbsp. finely chopped chives, plus more for garnish
- kosher salt
- Freshly cracked black pepper

Instructions:

1. Preheat broiler to 400°. Place peppers in a substantial preparing dish and heat 5 minutes.
2. In the mean time, beat together eggs and drain. Blend in bacon, cheddar and chives and season with salt and pepper.
3. At the point when peppers are finished heating, empty egg blend into peppers. Place back in the broiler and prepare 35 to 40 minutes more, until the point when eggs are set.
4. Trimming with more chives and serve.

Nutrition Information: Calories 91g: Fat 5.4g, Carbohydrates 5g, Sugars 3.3g, Fiber 1.6g, Protein 5g, **Points Value Per serving: 4**

LUNCH: CHICKEN CUCUMBER AVOCADO SALAD

Prep Time: 10mins, Total Time: 10mins, Servings: 6

Ingredients:

- 1 - Rotisserie chicken deboned and shredded skin on or off
- 1 - large English cucumber, halved lengthways and sliced into 1/4-inch thick slices
- 4-5 - large Roma tomatoes sliced or chopped

- ¼ - red onion thinly sliced
- 2 - avocados peeled, pitted and diced
- ½ - cup flat leaf parsley chopped
- 3 - tablespoons olive oil
- 2-3 - tablespoons lemon juice
- Salt and pepper to taste

Instructions:

1. Mix together destroyed chicken, cucumbers, tomatoes, onion, avocados, and slashed parsley in a substantial plate of mixed greens bowl.
2. Sprinkle with the olive oil and lemon squeeze (or lime squeeze), and season with salt and pepper.
3. Hurl delicately to blend the majority of the flavors through.

Nutrition Information: Calories 545g: Fat 38g, Carb 10g, Sugars 2g, Protein 40g, **Points Value Per serving: 23**

DINNER: EASY WHITE TURKEY CHILI

Prep Time: 5mins, Total Time: 20mins, Serves: 5

Ingredients:
- 1 - lb Organic ground turkey
- 2 - cups rice cauliflower
- 2 - tbsp. coconut oil
- ½ - a Vidalia onion
- 2 - garlic cloves
- 2 - cups full fat coconut milk
- 1 - tbsp. mustard
- 1 - tsp of: salt, black pepper, thyme, celery salt, garlic powder

Instructions:
1. In a substantial pot warm the coconut oil. Meanwhile mince the onion and garlic.
2. Add it to the hot oil. Blend for 2-3 minutes at that point include the ground turkey. Say a final farewell to the spatula and blend always until disintegrated.
3. Include the flavoring blend and rice cauliflower and mix well.
4. Once the meat is caramelized include the coconut drain, convey to a stew and decrease for 5-8 minutes, mixing regularly.
5. Now it's prepared to serve. Or on the other hand you can give it a chance to lessen significantly until thick and fill in as a plunge. Blend in destroyed cheddar for an additional thick sauce.

Nutrition Information: Calories 388g: Fat 30.5g, Carb 5.5g, Sugar 12.4g, Protein: 28.8g, **Points Value Per serving: 19**

Day 7

BREAKFAST: ZUCCHINI EGG CUPS

Prep Time: 10mins, Total Time: 40mins, Serves: 12

Ingredients:

- Cooking spray, for pan
- 2 - zucchini, peeled into strips
- ¼ - lb. ham, chopped
- ½ - c. cherry tomatoes, quartered
- 8 - eggs
- ½ - c. heavy cream
- Kosher salt
- Freshly ground black pepper
- ½ - tsp. dried oregano
- 1 - c. Pinch red pepper flakes
- 1 - c. shredded cheddar

Instructions:

1. Preheat stove to 400° and oil a biscuit tin with cooking shower. Line within and base of the biscuit tin with zucchini strips, to shape an outside.
2. Sprinkle ham and cherry tomatoes inside each covering.
3. In a medium bowl whisk together eggs, substantial, cream, oregano, and red pepper pieces at that point season with salt and pepper.
4. Pour egg blend over ham and tomatoes at that point top with cheddar.
5. Prepare until the point that eggs are set, 30 minutes.

Nutrition Information: Calories 114.8g: Carbohydrate 3.9g, Sugars 1.8g, Fiber 0.9g, Protein 8.5g, **Points Value Per serving: 3**

LUNCH: THREE INGREDIENT KETO STEAK SAUTÉ RECIPE

Prep Time: 10mins, Total Time: 30mins, Serves: 4

Ingredients:

- 1 - beef ribeye steak, sliced
- ½ - onion, peeled and sliced
- 2 - cloves of garlic, minced
- 2 – Tablespoons (30 ml) avocado oil, to cook with

Instructions:

Add avocado oil to a skillet and sauté the steak, onion, and garlic.

Nutrition Information: Calories: 798g: Fat 70g, Carbohydrate 7g, Sugar 3g, Protein 35g, **Points Value Per serving: 41**

DINNER: BBQ PULLED BEEF SANDO

Prep Time: 8mins, Total Time: 8hr 20min, Serves: 4

Ingredients:

- 3 -lbs Boneless Chuck Roast
- 2 - tsp Pink Himalayan Salt
- 2 - tsp garlic powder
- 1 - tsp onion powder
- 1 - tsp black pepper
- 1 - tbsp. smoked paprika
- 2 - tbsp. tomato paste
- ¼ - cup apple cider vinegar
- 2 - tbsp. coconut amino
- ½ - cup bone broth
- ¼ - cup melted Kerry gold Butter

Instructions:

1. Trim the fats off of the meat and slice into two huge portions.
2. In a bit, bowl integrates the salt, garlic, onion, paprika, and darkish pepper. At that point rub the whole thing over the meat. Place the beef in your slight cooker.
3. In any other bowl liquefy the margarine, rush within the tomato glue, vinegar, and coconut amino. Pour the whole thing over the meat.
4. At that point add the bone inventory to the slight cooker, pouring it around the hamburger.
5. Set on low and prepare dinner for 10-12 hours. Whenever finished, expel the hamburger, set the benefit lower back cooker to excessive and let the sauce thicken.
6. Shred the beef at that point upload it back into the moderate cooker and hurl with sauce. Serve

Nutrition Information: Calories 184g: Fat 15.1g, Carb 3.6g, Sugar 9.6, Protein: 5.1g, **Points Value Per serving: 10**

Day 8

BREAKFAST: BRUSSELS SPROUTS HASH

Prep Time: 10mins, Total Time: 40mins, Serves: 4

Ingredients:

- 6 - slices bacon, cut into 1" pieces
- ½ - onion, chopped
- 1 - lb. brussels sprouts, trimmed and quartered
- kosher salt
- Freshly ground black pepper
- ¼ - tsp. red pepper flakes
- 3 - tbsp. water
- 2 - garlic cloves, minced
- 4 - large eggs

Instructions:

1. In an extensive skillet over medium warmth, sear bacon till company. Kill warm temperature and alternate bacon to a paper towel-coated plate.
2. Keep most people of bacon fat in skillet, expelling any dark portions from the bacon.
3. Turn warm back to medium and upload onion and Brussels sprouts to the skillet. Cook, blending occasionally, until the point while the greens start to lessen and turn splendid.
4. Season with salt, pepper, and pink pepper portions.
5. Include 2 tablespoons of water and cowl the skillet. Cook until the factor that the Brussels grows are delicate and the water has dissipated round five minutes. (On the off danger that all the water vanishes earlier than the Brussels grows are sensitive, add greater water to the skillet and cowl for numerous minutes greater.)
6. Add garlic to skillet and cook until aromatic, 1 minute.
7. Utilizing a timber spoon, make 4 openings in the hash to find base of skillet. Break an egg into every hole and season every egg with salt and pepper.
8. Supplant pinnacle and cook dinner till the point whilst eggs are cooked to your loving, around five minutes for a in reality runny egg.
9. Sprinkle cooked bacon bits over the whole skillet. Serve heat.

Nutrition Information: Calories 350.1g: Fat 27.3g, Carbohydrates 14.8g, Sugar 3.9g, Fiber 5.9g, Protein 15.2g, **Points Value Per serving: 19**

LUNCH: KETO CARROT CHILI RECIPE

Prep Time: 10mins, Total Time: 1hr 25mins, Serves: 3

Ingredients:

- 2 - Tablespoons (30 ml) avocado oil, to cook with
- 1.5 - lb (675 g) ground beef
- 4 - slices of bacon, diced
- ½ - onion, diced
- 2 - carrots, shredded
- 2 - tomatoes, diced
- ¼ - cup (60 ml) water
- 2 - cloves of garlic, finely diced or minced
- ¼ - cup cilantro, chopped
- Salt and pepper, to taste

Instructions:

1. Add avocado oil to a considerable pot and dull hued the ground burger and bacon on high warmth.
2. By then include the onion and let it dim shaded for a few minutes as well.
3. Include the tomatoes and carrots and water.
4. Season daintily with salt.
5. Stew with the cover on for 60 minutes, mixing much of the time to guarantee it doesn't expend on the base.
6. Include the garlic and cilantro and cook for 5 minutes.
7. Season with additional salt and pepper, to taste.

Nutrition Information: Calories 440g: Fat: 37g, Carbohydrate 4g, Sugar 2g, Protein: 21g, **Points Value Per serving: 12**

DINNER: PORTOBELLO BUN CHEEsEBURGERS

Prep Time: 5mins, Total Time: 20mins, Serves: 6

Ingredients:

- 1 - lb. grass-fed 80/20 ground beef
- 1 - tbsp Worcestershire sauce
- 1 - tsp pink Himalayan salt
- 1 - tsp black pepper
- 1 - tbsp avocado oil
- 6 - Portobello mushroom caps, rinsed and dabbed dry
- 6 - slices sharp cheddar cheese

Instructions:

1. In a bowl, join ground meat, Worcestershire sauce, salt, and pepper.

2. Shape meat into burger patties.
3. In a vast dish, warm avocado oil over medium warmth. Include Portobello mushroom tops and cook for around 3-4 minutes on each side. Expel from warm.
4. In a similar container, cook burger patties for 4 minutes on one side and 5 minutes on the opposite side, or until wanted doneness is accomplished.
5. Add cheddar to best of burgers and cover with a top and enable cheddar to soften, around 1 minute.
6. Layer one Portobello mushroom top, at that point cheeseburger, wanted enhancements, and best with residual Portobello mushroom top.

Nutrition Information: Calories 336g: Fat 22.8g, Carb 5.8g, Sugar 12.2g, Protein 6.2g, **Points Value Per serving: 17**

Day 9

BREAKFAST: BACON AVOCADO BOMBS

Prep Time: 10mins, Total Time: 20mins, Serves: 4

Ingredients:
- 2 avocados
- 1/3 c. shredded Cheddar
- 8 slices bacon

Instructions:

1. Warmth grill and line a little heating sheet with thwart.
2. Cut every avocado into equal parts and expel the pits. Peel the skin off of every avocado.
3. Fill two of the parts with cheddar, at that point supplant with the other avocado parts. Wrap every avocado with 4 cuts of bacon.
4. Place bacon-wrapped avocados on the readied heating sheet and sear until the point when the bacon is fresh to finish everything, around 5 minutes.
5. Carefully, flip the avocado utilizing tongs and keep on cooking until fresh all finished, around 5 minutes for every side.
6. Cut down the middle across and serve instantly.

Nutrition Information: Calories 255.4g: Fat 13.1g, Carbohydrate 5.6g, Sugars 0.3g, Fiber 3.2g, Protein 29.1g, **Points Value Per serving: 8**

LUNCH: CAULIFLOWER MAC AND CHEESE

Prep Time: 10mins, Total Time: 30mins, Servings: 4

Ingredients:

- ½ - teaspoon kosher salt
- 1 - large head cauliflower, cut into bite-size pieces
- 1 - cup heavy cream
- 2 - ounces cream cheese
- 2 - teaspoons Dijon mustard
- 2 - cups shredded sharp cheddar, divided
- ¼ - teaspoon freshly ground black pepper
- 1/8 - teaspoon garlic powder

Instructions:

1. Preheat stove to 375 degrees F.
2. Heat an extensive pot of water to the point of boiling. Season the water with salt.
3. Splash a 8x8 preparing dish with vegetable oil shower.
4. Cook the cauliflower in the bubbling water until fresh delicate, around 5 minutes. Deplete well and place once again into the hot pot for a couple of minutes. Exchange the cauliflower to the preparing dish and put aside.
5. Get the cream to a stew a little pan, and speed in the cream cheddar and mustard until smooth.
6. Blend in 1/2 measures of the cheddar, salt, pepper, and garlic and whisk just until the point when the cheddar softens around 1 to 2 minutes. Salt and pepper to taste.
7. Expel from warm, pour over the cauliflower, and mix to join.
8. Top with the rest of the 1/2 glass cheddar and heat until sautéed and bubbly, around 15 minutes.
9. Permit to cool around 5 minutes at that point serve.

Nutrition Information: Calories 263g: Fat 20.9g, Carb 13.1g, Sugars 5.1g, Protein 9.5g, **Points Value Per serving: 13**

DINNER: DELICIOUS LOW CARB KETO MEATLOAF

Prep Time: 10mins, Total Time: 1hr, Serve: 6

Ingredients:

- 2 - pounds lean grass fed ground beef
- ½ - tablespoon fine Himalayan salt
- 1 - teaspoon black pepper
- ¼ - cup Nutritional Yeast
- 2 - large eggs
- 2 - tablespoons avocado oil
- 1 - tablespoon lemon zest
- ¼ - cup chopped parsley
- ¼ - cup chopped fresh oregano
- 4 - cloves garlic

Instructions:
1. Pre-warm broiler to 400F.
2. In a substantial bowl blend the ground meat, salt, dark pepper and nutritious yeast.
3. In a blender or nourishment processor blend the eggs, oil, herbs and garlic. Mix until the point when the eggs are foam and the herbs, lemon and garlic are minced and blended.
4. Add the egg mix to the meat and blend to join.
5. Add the meat to a little, 8×4 portion skillet. Smooth and level out.
6. Set in the stove, center rack for 50-a hour.
7. Painstakingly expel from the broiler and tilt the portion dish over the sink to deplete the liquid. Give it a chance to cool for 5-10 minutes before cutting into.
8. Topping with crisp lemon and appreciate!

Nutrition Information: Calories 344g: Fat 29g, Carb 4g, Sugar 8g, Fiber 2g, Protein 33g, **Points Value Per serving: 16**

Day 10

BREAKFAST: HAM & CHEESE EGG CUPS

Prep Time: 5mins, Total Time: 25mins, Serves: 12

Ingredients:
- Cooking spray, for pan
- 12 - slices ham
- 1 - c. shredded Cheddar
- 12 - large eggs
- kosher salt
- Freshly ground black pepper
- Chopped fresh parsley, for garnish

Instructions:
1. Preheat stove to 400° and shower a 12-glass biscuit tin with cooking splash.
2. Line each container with a cut of ham and sprinkle with cheddar.
3. Break an egg in each ham glass and season with salt and pepper.
4. Prepare until the point when eggs are cooked through, 12 to 15 minutes (contingent upon how runny you like your yolks).
5. Trimming with parsley and serve.

Nutrition Information: Calories 82.1g: Fat 5.2g, Carbohydrate 2.0g, Sugars 0.8g, Fiber 0.3g, Protein 7.1g, **Points Value Per serving: 3**

LUNCH: SALAMI AND CREAM CHEESE ROLL UPS

Prep Time: 10mins, Total Time: 20mins, Servings: 15

Ingredients:

- 15 - salami slices
- 1 ¼ - ounces cream cheese
- 7 ½ - teaspoons red pepper chopped
- 7 ½ - teaspoons banana peppers chopped

Instructions:

1. Spread about half teaspoon of cream cheddar on each cut of salami.
2. Spoon 1 teaspoon of red pepper on 5 cuts of salami.
3. Spoon 1 teaspoon of banana pepper on 5 cuts of salami.
4. Spoon 1/2 teaspoon of banana pepper and 1/2 teaspoon of red pepper on every one of the rest of the 5 cuts.
5. Overlay every one of the readied salami cuts like a taco and stay with tooth pick to keep shut.

Nutrition Information: Calories 153g: Fat 4.04g, Carbohydrate 0.61g, Sugar 6.1g Protein 2.88g, **Points Value Per serving: 6**

DINNER: KETO LOW CARB CHILI

Prep Time: 5mins, Total Time: 35mins, Serve: 6

Ingredients:

- ½ - tbsp avocado oil
- 2 - ribs celery, chopped
- 2 - lbs. 85/15 ground beef
- 1 - tsp ground chipotle chili powder
- 1 - tbsp chili powder
- 2- tsp garlic powder
- 1 - tbsp cumin
- 1 - tsp salt
- 1 - tsp black pepper
- 1 15 - oz. can no-salt-added tomato sauce
- 1 16.2 -oz. container Kettle & Fire Beef Bone Broth

Instructions:

1. In a substantial pot, warm avocado oil over medium warmth. Include slashed celery and cook until mellowed, around 3-4 minutes. Exchange celery to isolate bowl and put aside.
2. In same pot, include meat and flavors and dark colored hamburger until cooked all through.
3. Lower warmth to medium-low, includes tomato sauce and hamburger bone juices to cooked meat, and stew secured for 10 minutes, blending sporadically.
4. Add celery back to pot and blend until very much joined.
5. Embellishment, serves, and appreciates!

Nutrition Information: Calories 359g: Fat 22.8g, Carbohydrate 6.7g, Sugar 13.4g Protein 34.4g, **Points Value Per serving: 16**

Day 11

BREAKFAST: KETO FAT BOMBS

Prep Time: 5mins, Total Time: 25mins, Serve: 8

Ingredients:
- 8 - oz. cream cheese, softened to room temperature
- ½ - c. keto-friendly peanut butter
- ¼ - c. coconut oil, plus 2 tbsp.
- 1 - tsp. kosher salt
- 1 - c. keto-friendly dark chocolate chips

Instructions:

1. Line a bit heating sheet with fabric paper. In a medium bowl, consolidate cream cheddar, nutty spread, ¼ c coconut oil, and salt. Utilizing a hand blender, beat combination till absolutely consolidated around 2 minutes. Place bowl in cooler to solidify somewhat, 10 to fifteen minutes.
2. At the factor when nutty spread mixture has solidified, make use of a little deal with scoop or spoon to make golfing ball measured balls.
3. Place in the cooler to solidify, 5 minutes.
4. Then, make chocolate sprinkle: join chocolate chips and closing coconut oil in a microwave secure bowl and microwave in 30 2nd interims till completely softened.
5. Sprinkle over nutty unfold balls and vicinity returned inside the cooler to solidify, 5 minutes. Serve.

6. To save, keep shrouded in the icebox.

Nutrition Information: Calories 93.0g: Fat 9.7g, Carbohydrate 2.3g, Sugars 0.3g, Fiber 1.1g, Protein 1.2g, **Points Value Per serving: 5**

LUNCH: ITALIAN SUB ROLL-UP GRAIN-FREE

Time: Prep Time: 5mins, Total Time: 15mins, Servings: 4

Ingredients:

- 4 - Slices Genoa Salami
- 4 - Slices Mortadella
- 4 - Slices Sopressata
- 4 - Slices Pepperoni
- 4 - Slices Provolone overlook for sans dairy choice
- Paleo Lime Mayo or store-branch mayo we adore Chosen Foods Avocado Oil Mayo
- Shredded Lettuce
- Extra fixings our top choices are banana peppers, jalapeño peppers, simmered red peppers, and dark olives, if wanted
- Avocado Oil or Olive Oil
- Apple Cider Vinegar
- Italian Seasoning
- Toothpicks

Instructions:

1. Layer the beef cuts from largest to littlest. For the emblem make use of Boar's Head, the request is:

    - Genoa Salami
    - Mortadella
    - Sopressata
    - Pepperoni

2. Spread a skinny layer of mayo at the stack, creating a factor to leave the area at the very best point of the largest piece to defend it from squishing out whilst you flow them up.
3. Include a cut of provolone exceptional of the mayo, about most of the way from the fine. Include a touch bunch of lettuce to the decrease half and best with wanted garnishes Have the toothpicks adjoining and prepared to get. Beginning from the base of the cheddar, delicately (yet as firmly as attainable roll the stack, pushing in any fillings that find out.

4. When you get to the cease, secure the external meat edges with a toothpick.
5. To serve, pour 2 sections oil and 1 phase vinegar into a bit plunging ramekin.
6. Sprinkle a few Italian flavoring to finish the whole lot. Dunk the roll within the oil/vinegar and appreciate!
7. Store extra gadgets within the cooler, enveloped solely with the aid of saran wrap, for as much as seven days. These make for flavorful and simple school snacks.

Nutrition Information: Calories 234.3g: Fat 20.6g, Carb 0.9g, Sugar 14.4g, Protein 10g, **Points Value Per serving: 13**

DINNER: SUPERFOOD MEATBALLS

Prep Time: 10mins, Total Time: 50mins, Serve: 10

Ingredients:

- 3 -lbs 85% lean grass fed ground beef
- 1 -lb pastured chicken livers
- 1 - large shallot
- 4 - medium carrots
- 3 - garlic cloves
- 2 - tbsp. grass fed butter
- 1 - tsp dried oregano
- 2 - tbsp. coconut amino
- 3 - tsp salt
- 2 - tsp black pepper
- 1 - tbsp. dried thyme
- 1 - tbsp. garlic powder
- Olive oil

Instructions:

1. Warmth an expansive forged press skillet on medium warmth. While it warms, mince the shallots, carrots, and garlic until first-class. At the factor whilst the skillet comes to temperature encompass the veggies and sauté until fragrant and sensitive, around 8 mins, mixing often.
2. Include the chicken livers along 1 tsp salt and dried oregano. Cook, mixing frequently till the factor when the livers are seared everywhere.
3. Include the 1 tbsp. Coconut amino and 1 tbsp. Apple juice vinegar and cook dinner until the factor whilst reduced and livers are cooked.

4. Expel from warmth, and let cool a few minutes. Exchange to a nourishment processor and heartbeat to the point that it might seem that ground hamburger.
5. At that factor exchange to a considerable bowl, to cool to room temp.
6. Pre-warm broiler to 425F. Add the floor meat to the bowl with the staying salt and something is left of the flavoring. Blend nicely. Shape 1 ½ inch balls, will make hard 30.
7. Shower olive oil everywhere all through the sheet box. With oiled palms, coat every meatball in a bit olive oil and also you cope with it to put it on the sheet box.
8. At that point daintily sprinkle them with the rest of the coconut amino.
9. Place inside the broiler; prepare dinner at 425F for five minutes. At that point flip the temperature down to 350F and prepare dinner a further 20 minutes earlier than expelling from the broiler.
10. These meatballs are ideal for dinner prepare or sustaining a set. Dunk them in a farm, heap on a few guar or sprinkle with lemon tahini sauce for a few additional fats

Nutrition Information: Calories 323g: Fat 21g, Carb 4.3g, Sugar 7.3g, Protein: 31.8g, **Points Value Per serving: 13**

Day 12

BREAKFAST: PALEO BREAKFAST STACKS

Prep Time: 20mins, Total Time: 40mins, Serves: 3

Ingredients:
- 3 - breakfast sausage patties
- 1 - avocado, mashed
- kosher salt
- Freshly ground black pepper
- 3 - large eggs
- chives, for garnish
- Hot sauce, if desired

Instructions:

1. Warmth breakfast wiener as indicated via instructions on the container.

2. Squash avocado onto breakfast wiener and season with salt and pepper.
3. Shower a medium skillet over medium warmth with cooking splash, at that point splash inside a bricklayer bump pinnacle.
4. Place artisan jolt cowl inside the focal factor of the skillet and ruin an egg internal.
5. Place egg over overwhelmed avocado. Embellishment with chives, sprinkle along with your maximum cherished warm sauce and serve.

Nutrition Information: Calories 330g: Fat 13g, Carbohydrates 27g, Sugars 11g, Fiber 4g, Protein 26g, **Points Value Per serving: 15**

LUNCH: ANTIPASTO SALAD RECIPE

Prep Time: 10mins, Total Time: 10mins, Servings: 3 - 4

Ingredients:

- 1 - large head or 2 hearts romaine chopped
- 4 - ounces prosciutto cut in strips
- 4 - ounces salami or pepperoni cubed
- ½ - cup artichoke hearts sliced
- ½ - cup olives mix of black and green
- ½ - cup hot or sweet peppers pickled or roasted
- Italian dressing to taste

Instructions:

1. Consolidate all fixings in an extensive plate of mixed greens bowl. Hurl with Italian dressing.

Nutrition Information: Calories 462g: Fat 41g, Carb 7g, Sugars 2g, Protein 14g, **Points Value Per serving: 24**

DINNER: ROASTED CHICKEN STACKS

Prep Time: 10mins, Total Time: 50mins, Serve: 5

Ingredients:

- 5 - small chicken breasts
- 1 - head of Savoy cabbage
- 5 - slices of prosciutto
- 3 - tbsp. coconut flour

- 2 - tsp salt, more to taste
- 1 - tsp black pepper
- 2 - tsp Italian herb blend
- ½ - cup bone broth
- ¼ - cup avocado oil

Instructions:

1. Pre-warm stove to 400F.
2. Consolidate the chicken bosom, salt, pepper, herbs and coconut flour in a gallon measured plastic pack. Shake to equally coat the chicken, indeed, similar to shake and heat!
3. Shower a tbsp. of the oil on the sheet dish.
4. Shred the Savoy cabbage and make 5 little heaps of destroyed cabbage on the sheet dish. Sprinkle with somewhat salt. Shower a little oil on them. Place a covered chicken bosom over every one. In conclusion top every chicken piece with a cut of prosciutto. Shower with residual oil.
5. Broil at 400F for 30 minutes
6. Pour the stock in to the sheet skillet. Broil for an additional 10 minutes.
7. Expel from the stove and serve hot.
8. Utilize a spatula to gather up one stack at any given moment.

Nutrition Information: Calories 369g: Fat 24.8g, Carb 5.8g, Sugar 10.1g, Protein 33.7g, **Points Value Per serving: 16**

Day 13

BREAKFAST: HAM & CHEESE BREAKFAST ROLL-UPS

Prep Time: 20mins, Total Time: 40mins, Serves: 2

Ingredients:

- 4 - large eggs
- ¼ - c. milk
- 2 - tbsp. Chopped chives
- kosher salt
- Freshly ground black pepper
- 1 - tbsp. butter
- 1 - c. shredded cheddar, divided
- 4 - slices ham

Instructions:

1. In a medium bowl, whisk together eggs, drain, and chives. Season with salt and pepper.
2. In a medium skillet over medium warm temperature, liquefy unfold.
3. Pour half of the egg combo into the skillet, shifting to make a thin layer that covers the complete dish.
4. Cook for two minutes. Include half of the box cheddar and cover for 2 minutes greater, until the point whilst the cheddar, is melt.
5. Evacuate onto a plate, put 2 cups of ham, and roll firmly. Rehash with residual fixings and serve.

Nutrition Information: Calories 978.9g: Fat 72.6g, Carbohydrate 10.1g, Sugars 5.1g, Fiber 0.7g, Protein 70.5g, **Points Value Per serving: 44**

LUNCH: LOADED CAULIFLOWER BAKE

Time: Prep Time: 15mins, Total Time: 1hr, Serve: 4

Ingredients:

- 1 - large head cauliflower, cut into florets
- 2 - tbsp. butter
- 1 - cup heavy cream
- 2 - oz. cream cheese
- 1 ¼ - cup shredded sharp cheddar cheese, separated
- Salt and pepper to taste
- 6 - slices bacon, cooked and crumbled
- ¼ - cup chopped green onions

Instructions:

1. Preheat stove to 350 degrees.
2. In a substantial pot of bubbling water, whiten cauliflower florets for 2 minutes. Deplete cauliflower.
3. In a medium pot, liquefy together margarine, overwhelming cream, cream cheddar, 1 measure of destroyed cheddar, salt, and pepper until very much joined.
4. In a preparing dish, include cauliflower florets, cheddar sauce, everything except 1 tbsp.
5. Disintegrated bacon, and everything except 1 tbsp. green onions. Mix together.

6. Top with staying destroyed cheddar, disintegrated bacon, and green onions.
7. Prepare until the point that cheddar is bubbly and brilliant and cauliflower is delicate, around 30 minutes.
8. Serve quickly and appreciate

Nutrition Information: Calories: 498g: Fat: 45g, Carb 5.8g, Sugar 20.6g Protein 13.9g, **Points Value Per serving: 29**

DINNER: CURRY CHICKEN LETTUCE WRAPS

Prep Time: 5mins, Total Time: 20mins, Serves: 2

Ingredients:

- 1 - lb boneless skinless chicken thighs
- ¼ - cup minced onion
- 2 - garlic cloves, minced
- 2 - tsp Curry Powder
- 1 ½ - tsp pink Himalayan salt
- 1 - tsp black pepper
- 3 - tbsp. ghee
- 1 - cup cauliflower rice
- 6-8 - small lettuce leaves
- ¼ - cup Lactose free sour cream, unsweetened coconut milk yogurt

Instructions:

1. Set up your veggies and placed apart.
2. Cut your fowl thighs into 1-inch portions.
3. Warmth a large skillet on medium warm temperature. With regards to temperature encompass 2 tbsp. Of ghee and afterward the onion.
4. Blend frequently till cooked.
5. Include the bird, garlic, and salt. Blend nicely.
6. Cook the bird, mixing regularly until sautéed, around eight minutes.
7. Include the 1/3 tablespoon of ghee, the curry, and the cauliflower rice. Sauté until the point that everyone around joined.
8. Spread out your lettuce leaves, and spoon the curry bird combination into each one.
9. Top with a piece of cream

Nutrition Information: Calories 554g: Fat 36.4g, Carb 7.2g, Sugar 15.5g, Protein 50.9g, **Points Value Per serving: 26**

Day 14

BREAKFAST: BACON EGG AND CHEESE ROLL-UPS

Prep Time: 20mins, Total Time: 40mins, Serves: 6

Ingredients:
- 6 - large eggs
- 2 - tbsp. milk
- ¼ - tsp. garlic powder
- kosher salt
- Freshly ground black pepper
- 1 - tbsp. butter
- 1 - tbsp. chopped fresh chives
- 18 - slices bacon
- 2 - c. shredded Cheddar

Instructions:
1. In a substantial bowl, whisk together eggs, drain, and garlic powder and season with salt and pepper.
2. In a nonstick skillet over medium warmth, dissolve margarine. Include eggs and scramble, 3 minutes; at that point mix in chives.
3. On a cutting board, spread out three pieces of bacon. Sprinkle the base third with cheddar and best with a substantial spoonful of fried eggs.
4. Move up firmly. Rehash with outstanding cheddar and eggs.
5. Return skillet to warmth and include bacon roll-ups crease side down. Cook until firm on all sides, at that point exchange to a paper towel-lined plate to deplete fat. Serve.

Nutrition Information: Calories 279.2G: Fat 13.2g, Carbohydrates 28.7g, Sugar 5.1g, Fiber 1.5g, Protein 11g, **Points Value Per serving: 15**

LUNCH: MINUTE KETO SALAMI SALAD RECIPE

Prep Time: 5mins, Total Time: 5mins, Serves: 4

Ingredients:

- 100 - g or 3.5 oz salami slices
- 2 - cups (60 g) of spinach
- 1 - large avocado, diced
- 2 - Tablespoons (30 ml) olive oil
- 1 - teaspoon (5 ml) balsamic vinegar

Instructions:

1. Toss all the ingredients together.

Nutrition Information: Calories: 454g: Fat: 42g, Carbohydrate 10 g, Sugar 1g, Protein 9g, **Points Value Per serving: 25**

DINNER: LEMON BALSAMIC CHICKEN

Prep Time: 5mins, Total Time: 35mins, Serves: 4

Ingredients:
- 8 - boneless skinless chicken thighs (about 2 lbs)
- 3 - tbsp. pastured butter
- 1 - cup sliced onion
- 1 - cup shredded purple cabbage
- 2 - tbsp. minced lemon rind
- 2 - bay leaves
- 2 - tsp pink Himalayan salt
- 1 - tsp dried Italian herb blend
- 1 - tsp coarse black pepper
- 1 ½ - tbsp. balsamic vinegar
- 5 - tbsp. olive oil

Instructions:

1. Warmth your electric weight cooker on sauté mode. Include 2 tbsp. of margarine.
2. While it melts, peel and cut your onion. Proceed and prepare your lemon skin and your cabbage, as well!
3. Include the onion, cabbage and lemon to the weight. Sauté, mixing regularly until delicate.
4. Include the chicken thighs, seasonings and narrows clears out. Blend well and cook, caramelizing the chicken for a 2-3 minutes.
5. Pour in the vinegar. Drop the sauté work. Close the cover, select weight cook. Set it to poultry or high for 20 minutes.
6. When it has completed, let the weight discharges normally. Open the top, mix the chicken to shred. Blend in the last tablespoon of spread.
7. Spoon this tasty saucy chicken everywhere on your oodles, shower with olive oil or avocado oil! Appreciate!

Nutrition Information: Calories 325g: Fat 17.8g, Carbohydrate 6.9g, Sugar 12.2g, Fiber 4g, Protein 29g, **Points Value Per serving: 14**

Day 15

BREAKFAST: CLOUD EGGS

Prep Time: 15mins, Total Time: 20mins, Serves: 4

Ingredients:
- 8 - large eggs
- 1 - c. freshly grated Parmesan
- ½ - lb. deli ham, chopped
- Kosher salt
- Freshly ground black pepper
- Freshly chopped chives, for garnish

Instructions:

1. Preheat broiler to 450° and oil an extensive preparing sheet with cooking shower. Isolate egg whites and yolks, putting egg whites in an extensive bowl and yolks in a little bowl. Utilizing a whisk or hand blender, beat egg whites until the point when hardened pinnacles frame, 3 minutes.
2. Delicately overlap in Parmesan and ham and season with salt and pepper.
3. Spoon 8 hills of egg whites onto arranged preparing sheet and indent focuses to shape homes. Heat until gently brilliant, around 3 minutes.
4. Precisely spoon an egg yolk into focal point of each home and season with salt and pepper. Heat until the point when yolks are simply set, around 3 minutes more.
5. Topping with chives before serving.

Nutrition Information: Calories 106.2g: Fat 7.1g, Carbohydrate 0.7g, Sugars 0.2g, Fiber 0.0g, Protein 9.4g, **Points Value Per serving: 4**

LUNCH: KETO MUSTARD-SEARED BACON BURGERS

Prep Time: 10mins, Total Time: 20mins, Serve: 6

Ingredients:
- 4 - oz (110 g) of bacon, diced
- 1 ½ - lb (675 g) ground beef
- Salt and pepper
- 6 Tablespoons (90 ml) yellow mustard

Toppings:
- ½ - red onion, diced
- 1 - tomato, diced
- 1 - avocado, sliced

Sauce:
- ¼ - cup (60 ml) mayo
- 1 - teaspoon (5 ml) tomato paste
- 2 - teaspoons (10 ml) yellow mustard

Instructions:
1. Cook the bacon in a dish until fresh. Keep the bacon oil in the dish and place the bacon bits into a bowl with the crude ground hamburger. Season with salt and pepper.
2. Frame into 6 patties.
3. Sauté on high warmth the 6 burger patties – try to singe them to get incredible shading outwardly. You can likewise flame broil these.
4. Toward the end, spread 1 Tablespoon of mustard on every patty and burn the patty with the mustard-side down in the skillet.
5. To make the sauce, combine all the sauce fixings.
6. Spread a layer of sauce on every burger patty, and best with cuts of onions, tomato and avocado.

Nutrition Information: Calories 525g: Fat 45g, Carbohydrate 7g, Sugar: 2g, Protein 22g, **Points Value Per serving: 26**

DINNER: CREAMY MUSHROOM CHICKEN

Prep Time: 5mins, Total Time: 25mins, Serve: 2

Ingredients:

- 2 - pastured chicken cutlets
- 1 - small onion
- 5 - creaming mushrooms
- ½ - tsp pink Himalayan salt, more to taste
- ½ - tsp dried thyme
- 3 - tbsp. Kerry gold butter, unsalted
- 1/3 - cup full fat canned coconut milk

Instructions:

1. Warmth a cast press skillet on medium warmth. While it comes to temperature cut your mushroom and onions.
2. Once your skillet is hot, include two tablespoons of spread. At the point when dissolved include the cut mushrooms, sprinkle with ¼ tsp salt.
3. Sauté until seared, at that point include the onions. Continue mixing until relaxed, around 6 more minutes. Expel the mushroom and onion blend from the skillet.
4. Include the last tbsp. of margarine. Sprinkle your chicken cutlets with the staying salt and thyme. Place in the skillet next to each other. Cook for five minutes on one side. At that point flip over. Cook an additional 5 minutes.
5. At that point includes the mushroom and onion blends back in. Pour the coconut drain directly over it. Ensure you shake your can so you get a decent blend of coconut drain with fat.
6. Give stew for one moment, a chance to expel from warmth and serve! Idealize saucy protein to run with a major green serving of mixed greens!

Nutrition Information: Calories 334g: Fat 27.3g, Carb 3.2g, Sugar 14.2g, Protein 24.3g, **Points Value Per serving: 17**

Day 16

BREAKFAST: BUNLESS BACON, EGG & CHEESE

Prep Time: 10mins, Total Time: 20mins, Serves: 3

Ingredients:
- 2 - eggs
- 2 - tbsp. water
- ½ - avocado, lightly mashed
- 2 - slices cooked bacon
- ¼ - c. shredded Cheddar cheese

Instructions:

1. In a medium nonstick dish, positioned bricklayer jolt covers (focuses evacuated). Splash the complete dish with cooking shower and heat over medium warm temperature.
2. Split eggs into the focuses of the covers and daintily race with a fork to split yolk.
3. Pour water around the covers and cowl the skillet. Cook, giving the eggs a hazard to steam, to the factor that the whites are cooked through, around 3 minutes.
4. Evacuate pinnacle and satisfactory one egg with cheddar. Cook till the factor that the cheddar is particularly melt, round 1 minute more.
5. Modify the egg bun without the cheddar onto the plate. Top with beaten avocado and cooked bacon.
6. Top with the soft egg bun, cheddar face-down. Eat with fork and blade.

Nutrition Information: Calories 374.0g: Fat 29.1g, Carbohydrate 4.8g, Sugars 0.4g, Fiber 1.0g, Protein 22.6g, **Points Value Per serving: 17**

LUNCH: KETO CHICKEN COBB SALAD RECIPE

Prep Time: 10mins, Total Time: 15mins, Serves: 4

Ingredients:
For the salad:
- 1 - head of romaine lettuce, chopped
- 1 - tomato, diced
- 4 - slices of bacon, cooked and chopped into bits
- 1 - chicken breast, diced
- 2 - Tablespoons (30 ml) coconut oil, to cook chicken with
- Salt and pepper, to taste
- 2 - eggs, hard-boiled
- 1 - avocado, diced

For the dressing:
- 4 - Tablespoons (60 ml) red wine vinegar or lemon juice or lime juice
- 1 - Tablespoon (15 ml) mustard
- ½ - cup (120 ml) olive oil

Instructions:

1. Sauté the diced chicken bosom in the coconut oil.
2. Hard-heat up the eggs.
3. Cook the bacon and cleave it into bits.
4. Mix the dressing together.
5. Hurl every one of the fixings together with the dressing.

Nutrition Information: Calories 646g: Fat 62 g, Carbohydrate 7g, Sugar 1g, Protein 20g, **Points Value Per serving: 36**

DINNER: MUSHROOM BACON SKILLET

Prep Time: 10mins, Total Time: 20mins, Serves: 1-2

Ingredients:

- 4 - slices pastured pork bacon
- 2 - cups halved mushrooms
- ½ - tsp salt
- 2 - sprigs thyme
- 1 - tablespoon garlic comfit

Instructions:
1. Warmth an expansive forged press skillet over medium warm temperature

2. While it comes to temperature installation your fixings
3. Cut the bacon into ½ inch portions
4. Cut the mushrooms down the center
5. Expel the thyme leaves from the stems
6. Add the bacon to the skillet and prepare dinner until company at that point pass it to the aspect and encompass the mushrooms.
7. Sauté, mixing frequently until caramelized and starting to diminish
8. Include the salt, thyme, and garlic. Continue cooking, mixing regularly for an additional 5 minutes
9. Expel from the warm temperature while the mushrooms are terrific, scrumptious and shining in fats
10. Serve over veggies, with sensitive bubbled eggs or heap mix into a few heat juices

Nutrition Information: Calories 213g: Fat 8.5g, Carbohydrate 8.4g, Sugar 11.2g, Fiber 0.3g, Protein 13.6g, **Points Value Per serving: 10**

Day 17

BREAKFAST: HAM EGG & CHEESE ROLL-UPS

Prep Time: 20mins, Total Time: 35mins, Serves: 5

Ingredients:
- 10 - eggs
- 2 - tsp. garlic powder
- kosher salt
- Freshly ground black pepper
- 2 - tbsp. butter
- 1 ½ - c. shredded Cheddar
- 1 - c. baby spinach
- 1 - c. chopped tomatoes
- 20 - slices ham

Instructions:
1. Warmth oven. In an expansive bowl, split eggs.
2. Include eggs and scramble, blending at times, 3 minutes.
3. Blend in cheddar until liquefied; at that point mix in infant spinach and tomatoes until joined.
4. On a cutting board, put two cuts of ham. Top with a major spoonful of fried eggs and move up. Rehash with outstanding ham and fried eggs.
5. Place roll-ups in a shallow heating dish and cook until the point that ham is fresh, 5 minutes.

Nutrition Information: Calories 110.3g: Fat 4.3g, Carbohydrate 4.7g, Sugars 2.1g, Fiber 0.5g, Protein 11.8g, **Points Value Per serving: 4**

LUNCH: KETO SARDINES AND ONIONS RECIPE

Prep Time: 5mins, Total Time: 10mins, Serves: 4

Ingredients:

- 1 - can (3.5 oz or 100 g) sardines in olive oil
- ¼ - red onion, thinly sliced
- 1 - teaspoon (5 ml) apple cider vinegar
- 1 - Tablespoon (15 ml) olive oil
- Salt, to taste

Instructions:

1. Place the cut onions at the base of a bowl. Sprinkle with vinegar and olive oil.
2. Top with sardines.
3. Sprinkle salt, to taste.

Nutrition Information: Calories 385g: Fat 33g, Carbohydrate 3g, Sugar 1g, Protein 20g, **Points Value Per serving: 19**

DINNER: LOW CARB CRISPY KETO FRIED CHICKEN

Prep Time: 10mins, Total Time: 40mins, Serves: 4

Ingredients:

- 2 - tablespoons avocado oil
- 1 - cup sunflower seeds
- ½ - cup sesame seeds
- 1 - teaspoon fine Himalayan salt
- 1 - teaspoon ground black pepper
- 1 - teaspoon dried Italian herbs
- 1 - pound boneless skinless chicken thighs, about 8

Instructions:

1. Pre-warm broiler to 425F.
2. You will require an extensive Tupperware or cooler sack.
3. Oil a sheet skillet with the avocado oil.

4. Pound the sunflower seeds, sesame seeds and seasonings in a sustenance processor or powerful blender. Pound to a fine piece surface.
5. Add the prepared seed blend to a cooler pack or expansive compartment with a top.
6. Each one in turn add a chicken thigh to the pack or holder and shake until the point that very much covered at that point put it on the oiled sheet dish.
7. Rehash with the majority of the chicken.
8. Cook for 30 minutes, turning the chicken thighs over with tongs following 15 minutes.

Nutrition Information: Calories 463g: Fat 27g, Carbohydrate 7g, Sugar 13g, Fiber 3g, Protein 33g, **Points Value Per serving: 21**

Day 18

BREAKFAST: LOW-CARB BREAKFAST HASH

Prep Time: 10mins, Total Time: 50mins, Serves: 4 - 6

Ingredients:

- 6 - slices bacon, cut into 1" pieces
- 1 - onion, chopped
- 1 - red bell pepper, chopped
- 1 - large head of cauliflower, chopped
- kosher salt
- Freshly ground black pepper
- ¼ - tsp. smoked paprika
- 3 - tbsp. water
- 2 - cloves garlic, minced
- 2 - tbsp. finely chopped chives
- 4 - eggs
- 1 - c. shredded Cheddar cheese

Instructions:

1. In an intensive nonstick skillet over medium warm temperature, sear bacon until company. Kill warm temperature and exchange bacon to a paper towel-covered plate.
2. Keep the huge majority of bacon fats in skillet, expelling any darkish portions from the bacon.
3. Turn heat lower back to medium and include onion, chili pepper, and cauliflower to the skillet. Cook, blending from time

to time, tills the point that the vegetables begin to decrease and flip remarkable. Season with salt, pepper, and paprika.
4. Include 2 tablespoons of water and cover the skillet. Cook until the factor while the cauliflower is sensitive and the water has dissipated around five minutes. (On the off hazard that each one the water dissipates before the cauliflower is sensitive, upload extra water to the skillet and cover for two or 3 minutes more.)
5. Remove the cover, at that factor mixture in the garlic and chives and prepare dinner until the factor whilst the garlic is aromatic, around 30 seconds.
6. Utilizing a wooden spoon, make 4 openings in the hash to uncover base of skillet.
7. Break an egg into each commencing and season each egg with salt and pepper. Sprinkle cheddar and cooked bacon bits over the entire skillet.
8. Supplant pinnacle and cook dinner until the point that eggs are cooked for your enjoying, around five minutes for a absolutely runny egg. Serve heat.

Nutrition Information: Calories 334.6g: Fat 15.9g, Carbohydrate 30.0g, Sugars 2.2g, Fiber 3.7g, Protein 17.7g, **Points Value Per serving: 16**

LUNCH: CLASSIC KETO EGGS BENEDICT RECIPE

Prep Time: 15mins, Total Time: 30mins, Serves: 4

Ingredients:

- 8 - slices of ham
- 4 - eggs, poached
- 4 - slices of keto toast
- 2 - cups of spinach, steamed
- 2 - Tablespoons olive oil
- 2 - Tablespoons ghee

For the hollandaise sauce

- 3 - egg yolks
- 1 - Tablespoon lemon juice
- 4 - oz ghee, softened
- Salt and pepper, to taste

Instructions:

1. Gently sauté the ham and spinach in the olive oil.
2. Make the hollandaise sauce by whisking together the egg yolks and lemon juice. Place over low warmth and continue whisking ensuring the eggs don't cook.

3. At that point include the ghee, 1/2 Tablespoon at any given moment while you continue whisking. After you've included nearly the entire measure of ghee, the sauce should thicken to frame a thick, smooth sauce. Season with salt and pepper, to taste.
4. To assemble the eggs Benedict, spread the ghee over the 4 cuts of toast. Place 2 cuts of ham over each cut of toast.
5. At that point top with the spinach taken after by the poached egg and afterward the hollandaise sauce.

Nutrition Information: Calories 663g: Fat: 65g, Carbohydrate 2g, Sugar 1g, Protein 24g, **Points Value Per serving: 36**

DINNER: KETO ORANGE ROAST PORK LOIN RECIPE

Prep Time: 15mins, Total Time: 1hr 15mins, Serve: 4

Ingredients:

- 3 lbs of pork loin (1.4 kg)
- Juice from 2 small oranges
- Juice from 1 lemon
- Juice from 1 lime
- 3 Tablespoons of fresh rosemary leaves
- 5 cloves of garlic, sliced
- 3 Tablespoons (45 ml) of olive oil
- Salt and pepper, to taste
- 2 Tablespoons (12 g) paprika

Instructions:

1. Preheat stove to 400F.
2. Rub the pork loin done with olive oil and sprinkle with salt, pepper, and paprika. Rub the garlic and rosemary over the pork too.
3. Combine the juices.
4. Place the pork loin in a profound preparing dish and pour 1/2 of the juices over the pork.
5. Prepare in the broiler for 60 minutes. Like clockwork, pour a portion of the extra squeezes over the pork loin and flip the loin.
6. Expel from broiler when its inward temperature of the pork loin achieves 145F.
7. It'll continue cooking more after you take it out from the broiler.

Nutrition Information: Calories 359g: Fat 16g, Carb 7g, Sugar 4g, Fiber 2g, Protein 47g, **Points Value Per serving: 11**

Day 19

BREAKFAST: BACON WEAVE BREAKFAST TACOS

Time: Prep Time: 25mins, Total Time: 45mins, Serves: 4

Ingredients:
- 16 - slices bacon, halved
- Freshly ground black pepper
- 6 - large eggs
- 1 - tbsp. whole milk
- 1 - tbsp. unsalted butter
- kosher salt
- 2 - tbsp. Chopped chives
- ¼ - c. Shredded Monterey Jack
- 1 - avocado, sliced
- Hot sauce, for serving

Instructions:

1. Preheat range to 400° and line a significant, rimmed heating sheet with thwart. In one nook, make bacon weave with 8 parts of bacon each, making a rectangular. Rehash to make subsequent 3 weaves. Season with pepper. Place an altered heating rack on the pinnacle to make certain bacon lays degree.
2. Heat till the factor whilst bacon is a company, 18 to 20 minutes. Working swiftly, trim every rectangular with a paring blade or kitchen shears to make a round shape.
3. In the intervening time, make fried eggs. In a medium bowl, whisk collectively eggs with drain till the point when all round consolidated.
4. In a medium, nonstick skillet over medium-low warm temperature, dissolve margarine. Empty egg combo into the skillet.
5. Tenderly move the eggs around with a spatula, making significant curds. At the factor, while the eggs are distinctly cooked in your taking part in, season with salt and pepper. Overlap in chives and expel from warm.
6. Amass tacos: On a serving platter, fill the bacon taco shells with eggs. Sprinkle each with cheddar; settle in a couple of cuts of avocado, and quality with hot sauce.

Nutrition Information: Calories 540g: Fat 25g, Carbohydrate 10 Sugars 4g, Fiber 5g, Protein 20g, **Points Value Per serving: 22**

LUNCH: KETO HOMEMADE HAM RECIPE

Prep Time: 10mins, Total Time: 1hr 40min, Serves: 4

Ingredients

- 900g - smoked boneless gammon
- 1 - onion, peeled and roughly chopped
- 1 - celery stalk, roughly chopped
- 2 - garlic cloves, peeled and bashed
- 2 - teaspoons black peppercorns
- 1 - teaspoon whole cloves
- ½ - whole cinnamon stick
- ¼ - whole nutmeg
- ¼ - cup salt

Instructions:

1. Add each one of the fixings to a huge pot and cover with nippy water. Warmth the water to the point of bubbling, and use a spoon to skim off any foam to complete the process of everything.
2. Turn down the glow to a stew and half cover with a best. Guarantee the water doesn't vanish too quickly.
3. Simmer for a hour and a half. Oust the pot from the stove and let the ham cool in the liquid for a hour. Oust from the liquid and refrigerate for up to multi week.

Nutrition Information: Calories 112g: Fat 4g, Carbohydrate 0g, Sugar: 0g, Protein 20g, **Points Value Per serving: 3**

DINNER: KETO CROCKPOT SHREDDED CHICKEN

Prep Time: 5mins, Total Time: 6hrs 5mins, Serves: 4

Ingredients:

- 4 - chicken breasts
- 1 - cup chicken broth
- 4 - cloves garlic
- ½ - onion, sliced
- Salt and pepper, to taste
- 1 - Tablespoon Italian seasoning

Instructions:

1. Add everything to the Crockpot.
2. Cook on low for 6 hours.
3. Shred the meat with your forks.

4. Appreciate promptly in different dishes or stop in singular packs for sometime later.
5. Appreciate with Keto guacamole or over a serving of mixed greens with Keto Caesar dressing.

Nutrition Information: Calories 201g: Fat 10g, Carbohydrate 1g, Sugar 0.5g, Fiber 0g, Protein 24g, **Points Value Per serving: 6**

Day 20

BREAKFAST: EGGS AND VEGETABLES, FRIED IN COCONUT OIL

Prep Time: 5mins, Total Time: 10mins, Serves: 4

Ingredients:

- Coconut oil
- Spinach
- Frozen Vegetable Mix
- Spices.

Instructions:

1. Add coconut oil to skillet and turn up the warmth.
2. Include vegetables. For my situation, I utilize a solidified blend so I have to give it a chance to defrost in the warmth for a couple of minutes.
3. Include eggs
4. Include flavors. I utilize a zest blend, albeit salt and pepper work awesome as well.
5. Add spinach.
6. Panfry until prepared.

Nutrition Information: Calories 204g: Fat 20g, Carbohydrate 11g, Sugar 8g, Protein 35g, **Points Value Per serving: 10**

LUNCH: INGREDIENT KETO CHICKEN CURRY RECIPE

Prep Time: 10mins, Total Time: 35min, Serves: 4

Ingredients:

- 1 - lb (225 g) ground chicken
- 1 - can (400 ml) of coconut milk
- 1 - Tablespoon curry powder

- ½ - head of cauliflower, broken into small pieces
- 2 - Tablespoons (30 ml) coconut oil, to cook with
- Salt and pepper, to taste

Instructions:

1. Add coconut oil to a little pot and cook the ground chicken until insignificantly singed.
2. Incorporate coconut deplete, curry powder, and salt and stew with the best on for 15 minutes.
3. By then incorporate the cauliflower and cook for an extra 5 minutes.
4. Season with additional salt and pepper, to taste.

Nutrition Information: Calories 697g: Fat 55g, Carbohydrate 13g, Sugar 5g, Protein 42g, **Points Value Per serving: 34**

DINNER: VEGETARIAN KETO PIZZA RECIPE

Prep Time: 15mins, Total Time: 30mins , Serves: 4

Ingredients:

For the keto pizza crust:

- ½ - cup almond flour
- 2 - Tablespoons flax meal
- 1 - Tablespoon nutritional yeast
- 1 – Tablespoons olive oil
- 1 - egg, whisked
- Salt and pepper, to taste

For the pizza toppings:

- 1/4 cup (60 ml) Keto pizza sauce
- 2 Tablespoons (30 ml) cashew butter
- 1 Tablespoon (2 g) nutritional yeast
- 6 basil leaves, chopped

Instructions:

1. Preheat broiler to 400 F (200 C).
2. Combine all the base fixings to shape a mixture. Take off into a round level pizza covering.
3. Prepare for 15 minutes, deliberately flipping the outside layer following 10 minutes.

4. Blend the pizza sauce and cashew spread together. Spread over the pizza outside layer.
5. Sprinkle hacked basil to finish everything.

Nutrition Information: Calories 198g: Fat 16g, Carbohydrate 8g, Sugar 2g, Fiber 4g, Protein 8g, **Points Value Per serving: 10**

Day 21

BREAKFAST: SKILLET-BAKED EGGS, SPINACH, YOGURT, AND CHILI OIL

Prep Time: 10mins, Total Time: 35mins, Serves: 4

Ingredients:

- 2/3 - cup plain Greek-style yogurt
- 1 - garlic clove, halved
- Kosher salt
- 2 - tablespoons unsalted butter, divided
- 2 - tablespoons olive oil
- 3 - tablespoons chopped leek (white and pale-green parts only)
- 2 - tablespoons chopped scallion (white and pale-green parts only)
- 10 - cups fresh spinach (10 ounces)
- 1 - teaspoon fresh lemon juice
- 4 - large eggs
- ¼ - teaspoon kirmizi bibber (Turkish chili powder), or 1/4 teaspoon crushed red pepper flakes and a pinch of paprika
- 1 - teaspoon chopped fresh oregano

Instructions:

1. Blend yogurt, garlic, and a spot of salt in a little bowl. Put aside.
2. Preheat broiler to 300°. Soften 1 tablespoon margarine with oil in an expansive overwhelming skillet over medium warmth. Include leek and scallion; lessen warmth to low.
3. Cook until delicate, around 10 minutes.
4. Include spinach and lemon juice; season with salt. Increment warmth to medium-high; cook, turning as often as possible, until withered, 4– 5 minutes.
5. Exchange spinach blend to 10" skillet, abandoning any overabundance fluid.

6. On the off chance that utilizing 2 littler skillets isolate spinach blend similarly between skillets. Make 4 profound spaces in focal point of spinach in bigger skillet or 2 spaces in every little skillet. Deliberately break 1 egg into each empty, taking consideration to keep yolks unblemished. Prepare until the point when egg whites are set, 10-15 minutes.
7. Liquefy remaining 1 tablespoon spread in a little pot over medium-low warmth.
8. Include kirmizi bibber and a spot of salt and cook until the point that margarine begins to froth and seared bits frame at base of skillet, 1-2 minutes.
9. Include oregano and cook for 30 seconds longer. Expel garlic parts from yogurt; dispose of. Spoon yogurt over spinach and eggs. Sprinkle with spiced spread.

Nutrition Information: Calories 223g: Fat 4.9g, Carb10.3g, Sugars 2.4g, Protein 11.1g, **Points Value Per serving: 7**

LUNCH: KETO BEEF STUFFED PEPPERS

Prep Time: 20mins, Total Time: 20mins, Serves: 3

Ingredients:

- 1 - teaspoon of olive oil
- 2 - slices of bacon, finely chopped
- 1 - medium onion, peeled and finely chopped
- 13 - white button mushrooms, finely chopped
- 2/3 - lb of ground beef
- 1 - teaspoon of smoked paprika
- 3 - medium ringer peppers
- Salt and crisply ground dark pepper to taste

Instructions

1. Cut the completely off the toll peppers and oust all seeds. Carefully brush olive oil all in all pepper, all around. Set aside.
2. Preheat the stove.
3. Warmth the olive oil in a dish. Cook the bacon until firm. Oust bacon, keeping anyway much oil in the skillet as could sensibly be normal.
4. Add the onion and mushrooms to the oil and cook until fragile. By then incorporate the burger and paprika.

5. Cook until the point when the moment that the meat is caramelized. Season with salt and pepper. Remove from warm.
6. Scoop the meat mix into the ringer peppers.
7. Place the peppers on a plate and get ready for 20-25 minutes.
8. Trimming with cut parsley.

Nutrition Information: Calories 410g: Fat 3g, Carbohydrate 11g, Sugar 6g, Protein 21g, **Points Value Per serving: 12**

DINNER: ASIAN KETO CROCKPOT CHICKEN THIGHS

Prep Time: 5mins, Total Time 6hrs 5mins, Serves: 4

Ingredients:

- 8 - chicken thighs
- ½ - onion, sliced
- ½ - cup tamari sauce
- ¼ - cup water
- 4 - cloves garlic, minced
- Salt and pepper, to taste
- 1 - green onion, chopped for garnish
- 1 - teaspoon sesame seeds, for garnish

Instructions:

1. Place the chicken thighs at the base of the pot.
2. At that point include the cut onions, tamari sauce, water, and garlic. Endeavor to cover the majority of the chicken in the sauce.
3. Set on low warmth for 6 hours.
4. Season with salt and pepper, to taste
5. Enhancement with cleaved green onions and sesame seeds.
6. Roast the thighs in the broiler on a heating plate for 15-20 minutes to dark colored and fresh up the skin.

Nutrition information: Calories 434g: Fat 29g, Carbohydrate 4g, Sugar 1g, Fiber 0.3g, Protein 32g, **Points Value Per serving: 18**

Day 22

BREAKFAST: COWBOY BREAKFAST SKILLET

Prep Time: 10mins, Total Time: 20mins, Serves: 4

Ingredients:

- 1 - lb breakfast sausage
- 2 - medium sweet potatoes, diced
- 5 - eggs
- 1 - avocado, diced
- handful cilantro
- hot sauce
- raw cheese, optional

Instructions:

1. Preheat your stove to 400°F.
2. In a stove safe skillet, we utilized cast press, disintegrate and dark colored the hotdog over medium warmth.
3. When it's darker, utilize an opened spoon to evacuate the wiener and let it hang out while we cook the sweet potatoes.
4. Attempt to save however much of the oil as could reasonably be expected.
5. Hurl the sweet potatoes into the frankfurter oil and let them get fresh and cooked through.
6. Include the hotdog again into the skillet.
7. Make a couple of wells in the pan– one well for each egg. Split your eggs into the wells.
8. Place the skillet in the stove. We're simply heating the skillet sufficiently long for the eggs to set, around 5 minutes.
9. Presently, turn the broiler to sear and hit up the best side of the eggs for a couple of minutes, yet don't give the yolk a chance to cook the distance through– except if you don't care for runny yolks. Be that as it may, man, gracious man, the runny yolks run down truly pleasantly with the fresh sweet potatoes.
10. Expel the container from the broiler and splash the entire thing with avocado, cilantro and hot sauce.
11. Serve by scooping out an egg, alongside its neighboring treats, with a huge spoon.

Nutrition Information: Calories 1141g: Fat 90g, Carbohydrate 33g, Sugar 22g Fiber 4g, Protein 52g, **Points Value Per serving: 60**

LUNCH: KETO TURKEY BURGERS WITH JAMMY ONIONS

Prep Time: 10mins, Total Time: 30mins, Serves: 4

Ingredients:

- 3 - Tablespoons of olive oil
- 1 - medium onion, peeled and sliced
- 1 - Tablespoon of red wine vinegar
- 13 - oz of ground turkey
- 4 - slices of bacon
- salt and crisply ground dark pepper
- lettuce, to serve
- parsley, chopped to garnish

Instructions:

1. Preheat the stove to 320°F (160°C).
2. Warmth one tablespoon of olive oil in a dish. Cook onions on low warmth until delicate and jammy. Blend in red wine vinegar and put aside.
3. Season the turkey with salt and pepper. Separation into four vast patties.
4. Warmth two tablespoons olive oil in a dish and barbecue the patties on the two sides until brilliant.
5. Place patties on a cooking sheet and heat in stove for 15 minutes.
6. While the patties are heating, cook the bacon until firm. Put aside.
7. Serve the burgers on lettuce finished with the bacon and jammy onions. Trimming with hacked parsley.

Nutrition Information: Calories 734g: Fat 62g, Carbohydrate 7g, Sugar 4g, Protein 38g, **Points Value Per serving: 36**

DINNER: KETO MONGOLIAN BEEF RECIPE

Prep Time: 5mins, Total Time: 10mins, Serve: 4

Ingredients:

- ¼ - cup of avocado oil, to cook with
- 2 - cloves of garlic, minced or finely diced
- 1 - Tablespoon of fresh ginger, minced or finely diced
- 2 - beef steaks sliced
- 2 - Tablespoons of gluten-free tamari sauce or coconut amino

- 2 - teaspoons of white wine vinegar
- Salt and pepper, to taste

Instructions:

1. Add the avocado oil to a vast skillet over medium-high warmth. Include the garlic and new ginger to the skillet and sauté until fragrant, around 1 minute.
2. Add the steak to the skillet and sauté until cooked to your enjoying, around 3 to 5 minutes for medium-uncommon.
3. Include the tamari sauce or coconut amino and vinegar to the skillet and sauté for around an extra 1 minute. Season with salt and pepper, to taste.
4. Partition the hamburger between 2 plates and present with cauliflower rice.

Nutrition Information: Calories 789g: Fat 70g, Carbohydrate 2g, Sugar 0.3g, Fiber 0.2g, Protein 34g, **Points Value Per serving: 40**

Day 23

BREAKFAST: FLOURLESS EGG, COTTAGE CHEESE SAVORY BREAKFAST MUFFINS

Prep Time: 20mins, **Total Time:** 45-50mins, **Serves:** 12

Ingredients:

Dry Ingredients:

- ½ - glass almond feast (almond flour will most likely work, however I enjoyed the surface of the coarser almond dinner in this)
- ½ - glass crude hemp seed (see notes to perceive what I utilized)
- ½ - glass finely-ground Parmesan cheddar
- ¼ - glass flax seed feast
- ¼ - container healthful yeast drops
- ½ - tsp. preparing powder
- ½ - tsp. Spike Seasoning (discretionary yet great; can substitute any generally useful flavoring blend)
- ¼ - tsp. salt

Wet Ingredients:

- 6 - eggs, beaten
- ½ - container curds
- 1/3 - container meagerly cut green onion

Instructions:

1. Preheat broiler to 375F/190C.
2. Shower preparing containers or biscuit dish with non-stick splash or olive oil.
3. In a medium-sized bowl, combine the almond feast, crude hemp seed, Parmesan cheddar, flax seed dinner, nutritious yeast chips, heating powder, Spike Seasoning and salt.
4. In a littler bowl, beat the eggs and after that blend in the diminished fat curds and daintily cut green onions.
5. Blend the wet fixings into the dry fixings.
6. Scoop out the blend with a little estimating container and fill the biscuit mugs until the point that they are almost full, isolating the blend uniformly between the biscuit glasses.
7. Prepare for 25-30 minutes, or until the point that the biscuits are firm and pleasantly cooked.
8. These Flourless Egg and Cottage Cheese Savory Breakfast Muffins will keep in the refrigerator for no less than a week and can be warmed in the microwave or in a toaster stove.

Nutrition Information: Calories 259g: Fat 14g, Carbohydrates 16g, Sugars 10.5g, Fiber 4.8g, Protein 20g, **Points Value Per serving: 13**

LUNCH: KETO ZUCCHINI FRITTERS RECIPE

Prep Time: 10mins, Total Time: 30mins, Serves: 4

Ingredients:

- 4 - zucchinis floor
- 2 - inexperienced onions diced
- 2 - Tablespoons of onion powder
- 2 - Tablespoons of garlic powder
- 2 - teaspoons of dried oregano
- ¾ - degree of coconut flour
- 2 - eggs, whisked
- ¼ - degree of olive oil
- Salt and crisply ground darkish pepper, to flavor
- Tomato salsa, to serve

Instructions:

1. In the wake of pounding or sustenance setting up the zucchini, press out however much sogginess as you can by wrapping it by muslin and pulverizing as hard as could reasonably be expected. Pulverize to the point that you have a dry crush.
2. Join each one of the fixings beside the olive oil and tomato salsa. Edge into 12 lumps of around 1oz (30g) each. By then press into level patties.
3. Warmth the olive oil in a skillet and purposely put the losses into the hot oil.
4. By then, trade the abuses to a lubed warming plate and get ready in the stove for 10-15 minutes until totally cooked.
5. Present with a tomato salsa.

Nutrition Information: Calories 181g: Fat 12g, Carbohydrate 12g, Sugar 4g, Protein 5g, **Points Value Per serving: 10**

DINNER: KETO GROUND BEEF STROGANOFF RECIPE

Prep Time: 10mins, Total Time: 25mins, Serves: 3

Ingredients:

- 2 - Tablespoons ghee
- ½ - onion, diced
- 1 - lb ground beef
- 10 - mushrooms, diced
- 2 - cloves garlic, peeled and diced
- ½ - cup coconut cream
- ¼ - cup coconut yogurt
- 2 - zucchinis, made into noodles
- Salt and pepper, to taste

Instructions:

1. Add ghee to a pot and sauté the onion and darker the ground hamburger.
2. At that point include the mushrooms and garlic and sauté for 2-3 more minutes.
3. Include the coconut cream and stew for 10 minutes.
4. Season with salt and pepper, to taste.
5. Expel from warmth and include the zucchini noodles and blend in the discretionary coconut yogurt.

Nutrition Information: Calories 439g: Fat 37g, Carbohydrate 6g, Sugar 3g, Fiber 1g, Protein 20g, **Points Value Per serving: 22**

Day 24

BREAKFAST: SPINACH MUSHROOM AND FETA CRUSTLESS QUICHE

Prep Time: 15mins, Total Time: 1hr, Serves: 4

Ingredients:

- 8 - oz button mushrooms
- 1 - clove garlic, minced
- 10 - oz box frozen spinach, thawed
- 4 - large eggs
- 1 - cup milk
- 2 - oz feta cheese
- ¼ - cup Parmesan, grated
- ½ - cup shredded mozzarella
- Salt and pepper to taste

Instructions:

1. Preheat the broiler to 350°F. Crush the overabundance dampness from the defrosted spinach. Wash any soil or trash from the mushrooms, at that point cut meagerly. Mince the garlic.
2. Include the mushrooms, garlic, and a niche of salt and pepper to a non-skillet spritzed daintily with non-stick shower (or a sprinkle of cooking oil).
3. Sauté the mushrooms and garlic till the point while the mushrooms are delicate and most of the people in their dampness has dissipated away 5-7 minutes.
4. Coat a nine-inch pie dish with non-stick bathe. Place the clicking dried spinach within the base of the pie dish.
5. Place the sautéed mushrooms over the spinach, trailed by the disintegrated feta.
6. Season lightly with pepper. Pour the egg blend over the vegetables and feta within the pie dish.
7. Top with the destroyed mozzarella.
8. Place the pie dish on a heating sheet for easy move in the course of the broiler. Prepare the crestless quiche for 45-fifty five minutes, or until the point while the nice is splendid darkish colored (stoves may additionally change). Cut into six cuts and serve.

Nutrition Information: Calories 203g: Fat 11g, Carbohydrate 7g, Sugars 3g, Fiber 1g, Protein 16g, **Points Value Per serving: 8**

LUNCH: KETO ASIAN CHICKEN WINGS RECIPE

Prep Time: 10mins, Total Time: 45mins, Serves: 4

Ingredients:

- 2 - lbs chicken wings with skin on
- 2 - Tablespoons sesame oil
- ¼ - cup tamari sauce
- 1 - Tablespoon ginger powder
- 2 - teaspoons white wine vinegar
- 3 - cloves of garlic, minced
- ¼ -teaspoon sea salt

Instructions:

1. Preheat stove to 400 F (200 C).
2. In a huge compartment hurl the sesame oil, tamari sauce, ginger powder, vinegar, garlic, and salt.
3. Rush to altogether consolidate all fixings.
4. Add the chicken wings to the blend. Place the wings on a lined preparing sheet.
5. Prepare for 30-35 minutes until the point that the skin is firm. Sprinkle extra marinade on the wings part of the way through.
6. Turn on the oven for a couple of minutes on the off chance that you need it crispier.

Nutrition Information: Calories 277g: Fat 22g, Carbohydrate 1g, Sugar 0.4g, Protein 18g, **Points Value Per serving: 13**

DINNER: KETO CHICKEN "RAMEN" SOUP RECIPE

Prep Time: 10mins, Total Time: 10mins, Serves: 4

Ingredients:

- 1 - chicken breast, sliced
- 4 - cups chicken broth
- 2 - eggs
- 1 - zucchini, made into noodles
- 1 - Tablespoon ginger, minced
- 2 - cloves of garlic, peeled and minced
- 2 - Tablespoons gluten-free tamari sauce or coconut amino
- 3 - Tablespoons avocado oil, to cook with

Instructions:

1. Sear the chicken cuts in the avocado oil in an expansive griddle until cooked and sautéed.
2. Hard heat up the 2 eggs and cut fifty-fifty.
3. Add chicken juices to an expansive pot and stew with the ginger, garlic, tamari sauce.
4. Furthermore, include the zucchini noodles for 2-3 minutes to relax them.
5. Partition the juices into 2 bowls, top with the bubble eggs and chicken bosom cuts.
6. Season with extra hot sauce or tamari sauce, to taste.

Nutrition information: Calories 502g: Fat 37g, Carbohydrate 4g, Sugar 1g, Fiber 1g, Protein 30g, **Points Value Per serving: 23**

Day 25

BREAKFAST: COCONUT CHIA PUDDING

Prep Time: 10mins, Total Time: 20mins, Serves: 4

Ingredients:

- ¼ - cup chia seeds
- 1 - cup light or full-fat coconut milk, depending on preference
- ½ - tablespoon honey

Instructions:

1. Blend chia seeds, coconut drain, and nectar together in a little bowl or glass artisan bump.
2. Give it a chance to set in icebox medium-term.
3. Expel it from the cooler, and ensure your pudding looks thick and the chia seeds have gelled.
4. Top with crisp products of the soil, and appreciate promptly.

Nutrition Information: Calories 385g: Fat 21g, Carbohydrate 36g, Sugar 18g Fiber 22g, Protein 11g, **Points Value Per serving: 23**

LUNCH: KETO FLATBREAD RECIPE WITH NUTRITIONAL YEAST

Prep Time: 10mins, Total Time: 25mins, Serves: 4

Ingredients:

- ½ - cup unsweetened almond milk
- 1 - Tablespoon dried instant yeast or nutritional yeast flakes
- ¼ - cup coconut flour
- 1 - cup almond flour
- 2 - teaspoons baking powder
- 1 - Tablespoon garlic powder
- 1 - teaspoon Italian seasoning
- Dash of salt and pepper
- 1 - whole egg and 2 white eggs

Instructions:

1. Preheat the oven to 320 F.
2. Heat the almond milk up within the microwave for 40-5 seconds, then whisk inside the energetic dried yeast.
3. Set aside to cool slightly. The yeast will no longer be activated without the presence of sugar, so this step is purely to add a hint of flavor.
4. In a separate large bowl, integrate the coconut flour, almond flour, baking powder, garlic powder, Italian seasoning, salt, and pepper.
5. Check the temperature of the warmed almond milk as you do now not want to feature the eggs if it's far nevertheless too warm (else the eggs will scramble).
6. If you are happy it isn't too warm, whisk inside the egg and the two extra egg whites.
7. Add the moist aggregate into the flour combination and integrate well the use of a timber spoon. It ought to come together as dough.
8. Divide the dough into 6 small quantities and shape proper into a ball after which flatten them. Roll or press right into a flat oval form.
9. Bake for 12-15 minutes.

Nutrition Information: Calories 217g: Fat 12g, Carbohydrate 14g, Sugar 3g, Protein 11g, **Points Value Per serving: 11**

DINNER: KETO EGGPLANT AND BEEF CASSEROLE RECIPE

Prep Time: 25mins, Total Time: 55mins, Serves: 3

Ingredients:

- 2 - eggplants
- 4 - Tabs. of avocado oil
- 1 - onion
- 4 - slices of bacon
- 10 - white button mushrooms
- 1 - lb ground beef
- ½ - can of tomato sauce
- Salt and freshly ground black pepper
- Chopped parsley
- Sesame seeds to garnish

Instructions:

1. Preheat stove to 350 F (175 C).
2. Cut the eggplants lengthways as daintily as possible. Utilize a mandolin if it's simpler. You ought to have somewhere around 15-16 cuts. Disseminate the two sides with salt and put aside in a colander.
3. In a griddle, include 2 tablespoons of avocado oil cook the onions, bacon, and mushrooms until the point that the bacon is cooked.
4. Include the ground hamburger and cook until the point that the meat is caramelized somewhat, and season with salt and pepper, to taste.
5. Include the other 2 tablespoons of avocado oil into the skillet. Praise the eggplant cuts dry on the two sides and place into the skillet, cooking them on the two sides until the point when they are delicate. Do this in groups until the point when every one of your cuts is finished.
6. Oil a little preparing dish and tip in all the sauce.
7. Lay a delicate eggplant cut out before you on a slashing board and spoon a little sum on the end nearest to you.
8. Deliberately roll the cut up and put into the heating dish, settled in the sauce. Keep on doing so until the point when every one of the cuts are filled and rolled.

9. In the event that there's additional space of in the dish, at that point include any remaining meat blend.
10. Prepare in the stove for 20-25 minutes.
11. Serve scattered with hacked parsley and sesame seeds.

Nutrition information: Calories 425g: Fat 34g, Carbohydrate 14g, Sugar 7g, Fiber 6g, Protein 18g, **Points Value Per serving: 23**

Day 26

BREAKFAST: SMOKED SALMON EGG STUFFED AVOCADOS

Prep Time: 5mins, Total Time: 25mins, Serves: 4

Ingredients:

- 4 - avocados
- 4 - oz smoked salmon
- 8 - eggs
- Salt
- Black pepper
- Chili flakes
- Fresh dill

Instructions:

1. Preheat broiler to 425°F.
2. Divide the avocados expel the seed. On the off chance that the opening looks little, scoop out a little piece at any given moment until the point that it can hold an egg.
3. Orchestrate the avocado parts on a treat sheet, and line the hollows with pieces of smoked salmon.
4. Break every one of the eggs into a little bowl, at that point spoon the yolks and anyway much white the avocado will hold.
5. Include salt and new broke dark pepper over the eggs, to taste.
6. Delicately put the treat sheet in the stove and prepare for around 15-20 minutes.
7. Sprinkle bean stew chips and new dill to finish everything.
8. Serve warm.

Nutrition Information: Calories 480g: Fat 39g, Carbohydrate 18g, Sugars 2g, Protein 20g, **Points Value Per serving: 26**

LUNCH: KETO SHRIMP COCKTAIL RECIPE

Prep Time: 5mins, Total Time: 10mins, Serves: 4

Ingredients:

- 2 - Tablespoons Keto Tomato Ketchup
- 2 - Tablespoons mayo
- Salt and crisply floor dark pepper, to taste
- 8 - oz. cooked, peeled prawns
- 1 - glass ice shelf lettuce, destroyed
- ½ - gigantic avocado, diced
- Pinch Italian flavoring, to taste
- 2 - teaspoons lemon juice
- Lemon wedges, to serve

Instructions:

1. Combine the tomato ketchup with the mayo. Season with salt and pepper, to the flavor. Coat the prawns with this sauce.
2. Divide the shredded lettuce and diced avocado among cocktail glasses or bowls.
3. Then pinnacle with the prawns. Squeeze 1 teaspoon of lemon juice over every glass.
4. Serve with lemon wedges and sprinkle a pinch of Italian seasoning over the top of the prawns.

Nutrition Information: Calories 302g: Fat 22g, Carbohydrate 6g, Sugar 1g, Fiber 4g, Protein 24g, **Points Value Per serving: 14**

DINNER: KETO SLOW COOKER ROSEMARY LAMB MEATBALLS

Prep Time: 20mins, Total Time: 3hrs 20mins, Serves: 4

Ingredients:

- 14 -oz of ground lamb
- 2 - Tablespoons of olive oil
- 1 - medium onion
- 12 - white button mushrooms
- ½ - can of diced tomatoes
- A few sprigs of thyme
- 2 - sprigs of rosemary
- ¾ - cup of beef broth
- Salt and pepper to taste
- Cauliflower mash, to serve

Instructions:

1. Season sheep with salt and pepper and move into balls.

2. Add a large portion of the olive oil to a dish. Once warmed, sear meatballs until darker. Put meatballs aside.
3. Add the staying olive oil to a similar skillet and cook the onion and mushrooms until delicate and caramelized.
4. Exchange the meatballs and vegetables to the stewing pot. Pour in tomatoes, herbs, and juices. Cover and cook for 3 hours.
5. Enhancement with thyme leaves and serves on cauliflower crush.

Nutrition Information: Calories 441g: Fat 35g, Carbohydrate 8g, Sugar 4g, Fiber 2g, Protein 24g, **Points Value Per serving: 22**

Day 27

BREAKFAST: SAUSAGE AND EGGS TO GO

Serves: 4

Ingredients:

- 1 - pound Breakfast Sausage
- 6 - eggs
- 1 - green onion, cut
- Salt to taste

Instructions:

1. Preheat stove to 350°F.
2. Gap the wiener into 6 parts, and place each into its own particular individual ramekin.
3. Utilize your hands to push the frankfurter around the base and up the sides of the ramekin, making an "outside" for the egg to prepare in.
4. Split an egg into every wiener hull. For a mixed variety, whisk the eggs previously pouring in.
5. Top with a sprinkle of salt and a couple of cuts of green onion.
6. Prepare until the point when the eggs are set, around 30 minutes.

Nutrition Information: Calories 253g: Fat 21.8g, Carbohydrates 1g, Sugar 1g, Fiber 0.2g, Protein 12.9g, **Points Value Per serving: 12**

LUNCH: KETO THAI CHICKEN FRIED RICE RECIPE

Prep Time: 15mins, Total Time: 30mins, Serves: 4

Ingredients:

- 1 - head of cauliflower broken into florets and dried
- 8 - Tablespoons of coconut oil divided to cook with
- 3 - eggs, whisked
- 2 - chicken breasts diced
- ½ - medium onion peeled and diced
- 1 - medium bell pepper diced
- 2 - cloves of garlic peeled and diced
- 2 - Tablespoons of gluten-free tamari sauce or coconut amino
- 2 - teaspoons of fish sauce
- 1 - Tablespoon of fresh ginger minced
- Salt, to taste
- Cilantro for garnish

Instructions:

1. Cut up the cauliflower into little florets so they'll coordinate directly into a nourishment processor. Pat them dry on the off chance that they're wet so the cauliflower rice doesn't form into a mush.
2. Nourishment technique the cauliflower till it administration little rice-like pieces.
3. Include three tablespoons (forty five ml) of coconut oil directly into a skillet on medium warmth and include the three whisked eggs. Give the eggs a chance to cook a touch bit before mixing it.
4. Delicately blend the eggs as though you're making a scramble, anyway ensure the eggs don't cluster together an unreasonable measure of.
5. At the point when the eggs are very steady, put them aside.
6. Cook the diced winged creature in some other dish with each other three tablespoons (forty five ml) of coconut oil. Dark colored the diced hen and set apart.
7. Include 2 more noteworthy tablespoons (30 ml) of coconut oil to the skillet and cook supper the onions, peppers, and cauliflower rice on intemperate warmness. Sauté until the point when the cauliflower is diminished a bit.
8. At that point include back the chicken and egg and get ready supper for 1-2 minutes.

9. Include 2 tablespoons of tamari soy sauce and fish sauce, garlic, ginger, and salt to taste.
10. Cook for 2-3 minutes more prominent and serve. Topping with cilantro if favored.

Nutrition Information: Calories 535g: Fat 41g, Carbohydrate 11g, Sugar 5g, Fiber 4g, Protein 31g, **Points Value Per serving: 25**

DINNER: KETO BUDDHA BOWL RECIPE

Prep Time: 10mins, Total Time: 10mins, Serves: 3

Ingredients:

- 1 - large avocado
- 4 - cups of spinach
- 1 - small bunch of broccoli
- ¼ - head of cauliflower, food-processed into rice-like particles
- ¼ - cup shredded carrots
- 2 - Tablespoons of almond butter
- ¼ - cup of avocado oil
- Salt and pepper, to taste
- 2 - Tablespoons cilantro, chopped

Instructions:

1. Partition the spinach between 2 bowls.
2. Add the avocado oil to a skillet.
3. Sauté the broccoli for 2-three minutes on excessive warmth. Delicately season with salt and pepper, to the flavor. Separation and upload to the bowl.
4. Sauté the cauliflower rice on excessive warmth for a few minutes. Delicately season with salt and pepper, to the flavor. Separation and add to the bowl.
5. Include the destroyed carrots and cut avocado into the bowl.
6. Embellishment with slashed cilantro.
7. Shower with almond margarine to complete everything.

Nutrition Information: Calories 558g: Fat 52g, Carbohydrate 23g, Sugar: 4g, Fiber 14g, Protein 10g, **Points Value Per serving: 33**

Day 28

BREAKFAST: SPINACH, GOAT CHEESE & CHORIZO OMELETTE

Serves: 3

Ingredients

- 4 - ounces chorizo sausage
- ½ - Tbsp butter
- 4 - eggs
- 1 - Tbsp water
- 2 - ounces crumbled fresh goat cheese
- 2 - cups baby spinach leaves
- sliced avocado (optional)
- ¼ - cup salsa Verde (optional)

Instructions:

1. Expel chorizo from the packaging and broil in a medium sauté skillet until completely cooked.
2. Then beat the eggs and water in a little bowl.
3. Remove the chorizo from the skillet with an opened spoon and put aside. Wipe the container of the rest of the oil with a perfect paper towel.
4. Dissolve the margarine in a similar skillet over low warmth.
5. Add the beaten eggs to the container, at that point put the Chorizo, spinach, and disintegrated goat cheddar on a large portion of the egg blend.
6. Cook on low warmth for 3 minutes until somewhat firm, at that point overlap the unfilled side over the favor the filling on it.
7. Cover the skillet with thwart or a pot cover and leave on low warmth for an additional couple of minutes until the point that the eggs are cooked through.
8. In the event that your base is searing too rapidly, kill the stove and leave the dish concealed for to 10 minutes and the remaining warmth should "prepare" it until the point when the middle is completely cooked.
9. Present with avocado cuts and salsa Verde. So great you won't miss the toast or hash tans

Nutrition Information: Calories 324.1g: Fat 15.5g, Carbohydrate 26.7g, Sugars 0.4g, Fiber 5.5g, Protein 21.6g, **Points Value Per serving: 15**

LUNCH: KETO CHINESE FRIED RICE RECIPE

Prep Time: 15mins, Total Time: 15mins, Serves: 4

Ingredients:

- 2 - eggs, whisked
- ½ - large cauliflower, made into rice
- ½ - cup peas, defrosted
- ½ - cup carrots, grated
- ½ - cup leek, green onions and finely chopped
- 4 - oz chicken breast shredded and cooked
- 6 - Tablespoons avocado, coconut or olive oil and divided
- 2 - Tablespoons tamari sauce
- 1 - teaspoon sesame oil
- 1 - Tablespoon parsley or cilantro, chopped for garnish
- Salt, to taste

Instructions:

1. At that point, nourishment forms the florets with the aim that they frame little rice-like portions.
2. Include 2 tablespoons of oil right into a griddle on medium warm temperature and encompass the two whisked eggs.
3. Give the eggs a danger to cooking dinner a smidgen earlier than blending it. Tenderly scramble the eggs to shape little bits of cooked eggs. Season with a smidgen of salt. Put the eggs apart.
4. Get another griddle or smooth the alternative one and consist of 2 tablespoons of oil and prepare dinner the diced chook bosom. Put apart.
5. Include the ultimate 2 tablespoons of oil into a massive griddle. Include the cauliflower "rice" and green onions and allow it cool on medium warmth.
6. Blend robotically to make sure it doesn't consume!
7. Include the carrots and peas and cook dinner for five minutes.
8. At that factor lower back inside the chook and egg and prepare dinner for a couple of minutes more.
9. Season with the tamari soy sauce, sesame oil, and salt to flavor.
10. Cook for 2-3 minutes increasingly more and serve. Topping with parsley or cilantro if desired.

Nutrition Information: Calories 595g: Fat 54g, Carbohydrate 12g, Sugar 5g, Fiber 5g, Protein 22g, **Points Value Per serving: 32**

DINNER: KETO SHEPHERD'S PIE RECIPE

Prep Time: 15mins, Total Time: 1hr 45mins, Serves: 4

Ingredients:

- 4 – Tablespoons avocado oil, to cook with
- 1 ½ - lb ground lamb
- 1 - onion, peeled and finely chopped
- 2 - cloves garlic, peeled and finely chopped
- 1 - small-medium carrot, peeled and finely chopped
- 1 - celery stalk, finely chopped
- 1 - large sprig rosemary leaves picked and finely chopped
- 1 - sprig of thyme, leaves picked and finely chopped
- 1 - Tablespoon mustard
- 2 - cups beef or lamb stock
- ½ - head of cauliflower
- 2 - Tablespoons ghee melted
- salt and freshly ground black pepper
- 1 - teaspoon sesame seeds toasted

Instructions:

1. Warmth the avocado oil in a vast pot on high warmth. Include the ground sheep and onions and dark colored.
2. At that point include whatever remains of the vegetables, herbs, juices, and cook for 25 minutes on a low warmth until the point when the vegetables are mollified. Season with salt and pepper, to taste.
3. Meanwhile, bubble or steam or meal the cauliflower florets. Deplete if necessary to dispose of overabundance water and sustenance process with the softened ghee.
4. Season with salt to taste.
5. Blend into the sheep blend the mustard and afterward empty the sheep blend into a profound square or rectangular dish, packing down to minimal.
6. Top with the warm cauliflower pound and disperse over the toasted sesame seeds. Serve quickly.

Nutrition Information: Calories 640g: Fat 54g, Carbohydrate 10g, Sugar 4g, Fiber 3g, Protein 31g, **Points Value Per serving: 33**

Day 29

BREAKFAST: GROUND BEEF WITH SLICED BELL PEPPERS

Serves: 4

Ingredients:

- Coconut Oil
- Onions
- Ground Beef
- Spinach
- Spices
- A bell Pepper.

Instructions:

1. Cut an onion in little pieces.
2. Put coconut oil on dish, turn up the warmth.
3. Add onion to skillet, mix for a moment or two.
4. Include ground hamburger.
5. Include a few flavors (I utilize a zest blend, yet salt and pepper work fine).
6. Include spinach.
7. (Discretionary) If you need to zest things up a bit, include some dark pepper and stew powder.
8. Panfry until prepared, present with a cut chime pepper.

Nutrition Information: Calories 370g: Fat 18g, Carbohydrate 29g, Sugars 9g, Fiber 4g, Protein 25g, **Points Value Per serving: 18**

LUNCH: KETO SALMON FISH CAKES RECIPE AND CREAMY DILL SAUCE

Time: Prep Time: 15mins, Total Time: 35mins, Serves: 4
Ingredients:

For salmon fish cakes:

- 3 cans of salmon drained and flaked 2 Tablespoons of fresh dill finely chopped
- 3 medium eggs, whisked
- 1/4 cup of coconut flour
- 1/4 cup of shredded coconut
- 1/4 cup of coconut oil

- Salt and pepper, to taste

For cooking the fish cakes:

- 2 Tablespoons of coconut oil

For creamy dill sauce:

- 1/4 cup of mayo (60 ml)
- 1/4 cup of coconut milk (60 ml) (from a room temperature can)
- 2 cloves of garlic (6 g), minced or finely diced
- 2 teaspoons of fresh dill (2 g), chopped
- Salt and pepper, to taste

Instructions:

1. In a little bowl, race to consolidate the dill sauce fixings.
2. In a vast bowl, altogether join the fish cake fixings. Shape the blend into 8 patties.
3. In a huge skillet, soften 2 Tablespoons (30 ml) of coconut oil.
4. In bunches, precisely put patties in the oil. Cook until brilliant darker on one side and turn over and cook until brilliant dark colored, around 3 to 4 minutes for every side.
5. Serve the salmon patties with the smooth dill sauce.

Nutrition Information: Calories 600g: Fat 50g, Carbohydrate 5g, Sugar 1g, Fiber 3g, Protein 42g, **Points Value Per serving: 28**

DINNER: INGREDIENT CREAMY KETO SALMON PASTA

Prep Time: 5mins, Total Time: 5mins, Serves: 3

Ingredients:

- 2 Tablespoons of coconut oil
- 8 oz of smoked salmon diced
- 2 zucchinis spiraled or use a peeler to make into long noodle-like strands
- 1/4 cup of mayo

Instructions:

1. In a skillet, mellow the coconut oil over medium-high warmth. Incorporate the smoked salmon and sauté until to some degree burned around 2 to 3 minutes.
2. Incorporate the zucchini "noodles" to the skillet and sauté until sensitive, around 1 to 2 minutes.
3. Add the mayo to the skillet, blending commendably to merge.
4. Partition the "pasta" between 2 plates and serve.

Nutrition Information: Calories 470g: Fat 42g, Carbohydrate 4g, Sugar 2g, Fiber 1g, Protein 21g, **Points Value Per serving: 24**

Day 30

BREAKFAST: CHEESEBURGERS WITHOUT THE BUN

Serves: 4

Ingredients:

- Butter
- Hamburgers
- Cheddar Cheese
- Cream Cheese
- Salsa
- Spices
- Spinach.

Instructions:

1. Put margarine on skillet, turn up the warmth.
2. Include burgers and flavors.
3. Flip until near being prepared.
4. Include a couple of cuts of cheddar and some cream cheddar to finish everything.
5. Turn down the warmth and put a cover on the container until the point when the cheddar dissolves.
6. Present with some spinach. I jump at the chance to pour a portion of the fat from the dish over the spinach.
7. To make the burgers significantly more succulent, include some salsa top.

Nutrition Information: Calories 150g: Fat 10g, Carbohydrates 5g, Sugar 7g Fiber 0.3g, Protein 10g, **Points Value Per serving: 7**

LUNCH: KETO ROAST BEEF RECIPE AND CARROTS AND ONIONS

Prep Time: 10mins, Total Time 1hr 10mins, Serves: 4
Ingredients:

- 2 - lbs of beef round
- 2 - carrots peeled and roughly chopped
- ¾ - medium onion peeled and roughly chopped
- 6 - cloves of garlic peeled and lightly crushed
- 4 - Tablespoons of olive oil
- 1 - large sprig of rosemary
- 1 - sprig of thyme
- Salt and pepper, to taste

Instructions:

1. Preheat stove to 400 F
2. Hurl the carrots, onion, and garlic with olive oil, a portion of the rosemary and thyme, and salt.
3. Place in the focal point of a preparing plate.
4. Rub olive oil, rest of the rosemary and thyme, and salt on the meat round and put over the vegetables.
5. Broil for 60 minutes.

Nutrition Information: Calories 739g: Fat 62g, Carbohydrate 6g, Sugar 2g, Fiber 1g, Protein 38g, **Points Value Per serving: 37**

DINNER: KETO BACON GREEN BEANS RECIPE

Prep Time: 10mins, Total Cook Time: 25mins, Serves: 4
Ingredients:

- ½ - lb green beans
- 6 - slices of bacon, cooked and chopped into bits
- 3 – Tablespoons of avocado oil
- 1 – Tablespoon gluten-free tamari sauce
- Salt and pepper, to taste

Instructions:

1. Parboil the green beans in a pot of bubbling water. Bubble for 3-4 minutes until marginally delicate.

2. On the off chance that the bacon isn't concocted, slash it and cook in a skillet with avocado oil.
3. Include the depleted parboiled green beans to the skillet with the bacon and oil and cook until the point when the green beans fresh up marginally.
4. Include tamari sauce and salt and pepper to taste.

Nutrition Information: Calories 302g: Fat 30g, Carbohydrate 4g, Sugar 0.3g, Fiber 2g, Protein 7g, **Points Value Per serving: 17**

Conclusion

The recipes of this book don't appear labor intensive and the ingredients are easily found in any grocery store. Additionally, it has suggestions for substitutions within many of the recipes. Altogether, this is a quality addition cookbook and helpful for anyone who are like following the Weight Watchers plan.

Hope the book helps you to find an effective method for weight loss, healthy living while saving money.

Made in the USA
San Bernardino, CA
29 July 2019